Nourish in 5

Healthy desserts that are 5 ingredients, easy & delicious

By Amy Lee

Introduction

Cooking for our Future

Nourishing Recipes

Breakfasts

Cult Cookies

Bars, Brownies & Breads

Cakes & Cupcakes

Chocolate Cravings

Frozen 'n' Chilled

Nourish yourself everyday

Snacks

Sweet Sides

Thanks for picking me up,

and making the world a healthier, more delicious and more eco-friendly place!

Hello! My name is Amy, and I'm the girl behind the Nourish in 5 Cookbook, health blog, AMY LEE ACTIVE, and a Digital Marketing business called Digiteyes Media. I love healthifying my favourite foods, photography, strength training (no to cardio, sorry not sorry), eating Protein Peanut Butter Cups (page 162) post-workout, and feeding friends, family, and hopefully, yourself!

In much of my daily life, @amyleeactive on Instagram, and in this book, I share colourful healthy treats, a sustainable approach to eating more wholefoods, and tips for keeping active! This is not just a cookbook with healthy recipes. It's about connecting with loved ones, making memories, and being kind to yourself and the earth.

I love sleep
because it's
like a time
machine to
breakfast

Make every
recipe your
own

It's my life goal to make healthy eating accessible, affordable and delicious. Nourish in 5 is a dream come to life, a tool that will help me help you to make truly healthy desserts using only 5 nourishing ingredients, with a zero-waste approach.

I encourage you to make every recipe your own; with options to suit vegan, gluten-free, low carb diets and more! I do not count baking soda/powder, salt, vanilla and cinnamon in the ingredients, as these basics can basically be thrown into any recipe. I'm personally a self-confessed cinnamon addict, adding a pinch of this antioxidant-rich spice to anything and everything!

The recipes are triple-tested, designed to set you up for cooking success and to be versatile with multiple uses, so there's never any waste - for example, the vegan salted caramel recipes (on page 236) can be used across so many recipes in the book; Caramel Popcorn (page 222), 1 Bowl Vegan Brownies (page 116), on top of cookies, ice cream and cakes, or simply licked off the spoon...the possibilities are endless.

Each element of every recipe is 5 ingredients or less, so feel free to omit elements wherever you see fit.

**A PROUD
SUPPORTER
OF OZHARVEST**

Every Book Sold Feeds Someone In Need

This book proudly supports OzHarvest charity

This zero-waste approach to cooking is not only fun, it's also better for the planet we live in. There's enough food produced in the world to feed everyone to the brim, yet a third of all food produced is wasted. That is a whopping 1.3 billion tonnes of edible food that is thrown out, or $1 trillion each year.

I cannot stand food wastage when millions of people are malnourished and I know so many of you are the same – that is why I've chosen to support OzHarvest, an incredible charity whose mission is to nourish Australia by rescuing quality food that would have otherwise been discarded, to nourish those in need.

I truly believe that we can all do our part for the planet, however small those steps may be. I'm incredibly proud to say that every Nourish in 5 book sold will feed someone in need thanks to OzHarvest.

If you'd like to find out more about OzHarvest and help fight food waste, head to OzHarvest.org

Your support, in any size, shape or form, makes a difference.

Cooking for our future

10 Tips For Zero-Waste Cooking

The Nourish in 5 philosophy is all about recipes that are not only healthy, but made with zero-waste cooking methods and sustainable kitchenware. Every single person can play a role in working towards a more eco-friendly and health-conscious planet, however small those steps may be - every bit of effort counts!

1. Plan!

It seems obvious, but planning ahead is so often overlooked, and a lack of planning more often than not results in impulse purchases that you don't need. Check your fridge regularly to see what food you have, what's going off soon, what can be frozen, what veg is on the turn that can be made into a quick side dish or soup. Write a list, stick to it, and don't go to the shops hungry!

2. Bulk-Buy

Buying in bulk lessens your amount of packaging. If you are a small family, or solo consumer, buy with friends and divvy things up. Once you're home, transfer dry goods to glass jars, or food grade stainless steel containers and store in your pantry.

3. Reduce "Convenience" Foods

Try to reduce or eliminate your reliance on ready-made meals, as these come with an environmental price tag. Instead, try making as much of your own food as you can. Stock your pantry and fridge with your own DIY foods - jams, chutneys, muesli, snacks. You'll be surprised at how easy things are to make, after all, our parents and grandparents had much less fewer modern conveniences! Try the delicious Berry Chia Jam on page 228, the Nutter Butter Granola on page 39 and the Salted Caramel Coconut Chips on page 198 to get started on easy, healthy, delicious, affordable snacks!

4. Canned Food

Cans are an exception for convenience foods as they last a long time - look for cans that are BPA-free with NO additives, stabilisers, emulsifiers, thickeners, artificial colours, flavours and preservatives. with minimal ingredients. For example, I use Organic Road Coconut Milk which only contains organic coconut extract and water. You'd be amazed at how many cans have added nasties, so make sure to always read the label. Canned beans, tomatoes, coconut cream and milk are all great things to have on hand.

5. Support Local

Buy local produce wherever possible - they often retain more nutrients and are allowed to ripen naturally, while food that travels long distances is often picked before it's ripe. Try to pick food that is fresh and in season. When you consider the carbon footprint of transporting goods long distances to consumers, it makes total sense to buy your products locally.

6. Bring your own bags

Always keep reusable shopping/grocery bags and reusable fruit and veg mesh bags on hand - I like to leave some in my car aswell. Very easy way to eliminate plastic!

7. Keep Hydrated

In Australia, the quality of our drinking water is high, so it's a waste to purchase bottled water, as the impact of production and packaging is high. Instead in a reusable bottle to use on the go and break the cycle of dependence. The same goes for coffee cups for takeaway beverages, invest in a good quality, leak proof cup - such as this stainless steel cup from Made By Fressko, which keeps things cool or hot for longer.

8. Grow your own Fruit, Veg, Herbs

The only thing better than locally produced food is when you DIY your own produce in your backyard! Even if you don't have a green thumb, you can definitely keep a herb pot alive in your garden or kitchen window, and it's so much cheaper and fresher to buy the plant rather than buy packaged herbs from the supermarket.

9. Food Sources

Health food stores, some delis and independent retailers and green grocers are supporters of local, organic and sustainably produced foods, having the edge over major supermarket chains

10. Certification

Purchase organic and fairtrade wherever possible. Organic and Fairtrade certification labels on food are the shopper's sign for sustainable and ethically produced food. The international Fairtrade brand is granted to products that meet certain enviornmental, labour and developmental standards, important for farmers growing coffee and cocoa in third-world countries being guaranteed better prices for their crop. I choose Organic Road brand from Go Vita Australia stores.

Zero-Waste Kitchen

When it comes to eco-friendly, zero-waste cooking and cleaning in your kitchen (yes, cleaning is an essential part of cooking!) you'll be surprised at how easy it is to make these swaps in your home, and also how much money and resources you'll save! It is becoming widely known that single-use packaging, designed to provide us convenience, are actually an inconvenience to our health and our environment. Make these simple swaps today and your wallet and the planet will thank you.

SWAP: Plastic wrap | FOR: Beeswax wrap

Beeswax wraps are the perfect solution for single-use plastic plastic/cling wrap. Not only is it zero-waste, it keeps food fresher for longer with their antimicrobial properties. Unfortunately, plastic wrap isn't reusable and is rarely recycled as it can clog machinery. Swapping for beeswax wrap also saves money, as the average family uses 24 rolls of plastic cling wrap per year (Save yourself approximately $100 annually with this swap!). BUY FROM: Online from ENJO Australia (www.enjo.com.au) Made from biodegradable organic cotton sheets that are infused with beeswax, dammar resin and coconut and jojoba oils. They create a breathable, pliable material that replaces the need for plastic cling wrap. Simply warm the wraps with your hands so the wrap becomes malleable. Wash in soapy cold water and hang to dry. Easy!

SWAP: Single-use coffee cup & plastic bottles
FOR: Reusable stainless steel cup & reusable stainless steel or glass bottle

Take-away coffee cups and bottles are a burden on our waste management services and our environment, filling up landfills and resulting in transport emission. Contrary to popular belief, takeaway coffee cups are NOT recyclable and it takes 30 years for it to breakdown in landfill. An estimated one billion coffee cups end up in landfill each year in Australia alone. If you divide that over the course of the year, that's roughly 2,700,000 paper coffee cups thrown out every day. If stacked end-to-end, one billion coffee cups would stretch 120,000km, or three times around the world. Invest in an affordable, reusable cup and water bottle for coffee and hydration on-the-go - they're also much more stylish in reusable form! BUY FROM: Online from Made By Fressko (www.madebyfressko.com)

SWAP: Plastic storage containers
FOR: Glass and stainless steel

Try glass or food-grade stainless steel containers. You can also recycle glass jars that foods are packaged in, they make awesome affordable food storage options. BUY FROM: Supermarket, homewares shops, health food stores.

SWAP: Plastic Ice Cube Trays
FOR: Metal Ice Cube Trays

Stainless steel trays are the way to go over plastic, especially for baby food, and they also freeze contents faster. BUY FROM: Homewares shops, health food stores.

SWAP: Plastic Zip-Lock Bags
FOR: Reusable Hemp Bags

Hemp Produce Bags are available in a variety if sizes, resealable and made from breathable fabric. They're a great alternative for storing fruit, vegetable and herbs in the fridge. BUY FROM: Homeware shops, health food stores and online eco shops.

SWAP: Chemical Cleaning Spray
FOR: Kitchen Fibres

Whether it's the 'toxic' warning labels, the long list of strange ingredients that all seem to end in 'oxide', 'ethylene' or 'chlorite', or the strong citrus-like smell that lingers through your house, our household cleaning products don't give off a friendly vibe and are definitely not natural. For general kitchen mess after cooking, I find quality kitchen fibre cloths sprayed with plain water, do the trick - no chemicals needed! It's literally as simple as wet, wipe and dry - I use the ENJO Kitchen Glove for large surfaces (kitchen benchtops, cupboard doors), then dry with their Kitchen Miracle (sinks, bench tops, stove tops, cupboards, splashbacks). The fibres loosen and lift kitchen grease and grime with just water from a reusable Spray Bottle. BUY FROM: ENJO Kitchen Bundle from ENJO Australia (www.enjo.com.au) Kitchen Bundle replaces 18 bottles of all purpose spray, 9360 paper towel sheets, and 156 kitchen sponges/dish clothes over 3 years. All fibre purchases are also packaged in ENJO laundry bags. Old and used ENJO Fibres are recycled and reproduced into insulating material, furniture or car seat filling.

SWAP: Paper Towels | FOR: Bamboo Tea Towels

Long lasting quality tea towels can be used to mop up spills and pat foods dry. They can even be used as reusable gift wrap! If you have to use paper towels, be aware that they're compostable as long as they haven't been used to mop up anything greasy, such as oil or butter. BUY FROM: Bamboo T-Towels online from ENJO Australia (www.enjo.com.au)

SWAP: Single-Use Plastic Straws
FOR: Metal Reusable Straws

Australians use about 10 million single-use plastic straws every day. This adds up to a huge 3.5 billion a year – no wonder they are one of the most common items polluting our otherwise beautiful beaches and harming marine animals. It is estimated that 8 million tonnes of plastic pollute our oceans every year. We use plastic straws for an average of 20 minutes, but they stay around for approximately 600 years. So, when it comes to plastic straws, simply say no, or BYO reusable straw. BUY FROM: Health food stores.

KITCHENWARE

Purchase cooking saucepans and pans that can be taken from stove to table - it's perfectly fine to store food in a saucepan, as long as it's made from stainless steel. Avoid aluminium and uncoated cast iron, as food acids can react with the pan surface resulting in contaminated food. Try my Blueberry Friand Skillet Cake on page 127, even cakes can be served in skillets! (Just be careful when slicing not to cut through the non-stick coating of the pan).

ENJO Kitchen Range

ENJO Kitchen Glove

Beeswax Wraps

Pantry Staples

Whether you're an occasional or an everyday cook, these are the wholefoods pantry essentials you should never be without, and you'll need plenty of each for successful Nourish in 5 cooking! As mentioned, I recommend bulk-buying to reduce packaging and waste. I also recommend the best ingredients in grey, as those are the brands I've been using to (at minimum) triple-test the recipes, so I can safely vouch for their quality and success!

BASICS (not included in ingredient count):

salt, baking soda, baking powder, vanilla, and cinnamon. A pinch of all these generally make every recipe better, and if you really need to, you can omit them in any method in this book - you'll just have to be aware that they may not be the best they can be!

I personally would add a touch of vanilla and cinnamon to everything (even when it's not written in the method). I LOVE vanilla bean powder, which is a very concentrated flavour, however in this book I've written vanilla essence/extract, as this is more widely available and affordable. For every teaspoon of extract or paste, you can substitute for 1/2 teaspoon of ground powder. Cinnamon also contains large amounts of polyphenol antioxidants, which can be found to have anti-inflammatory effects, and the prebiotic properties can help improve gut health.

NUT FLOURS: my favourites are almond meal and almond flour, great for gluten-free, low carb and keto baking. I hear you asking what the difference is; they can be used interchangeably in recipes however the textural results will be different. Almond meal is whole almonds ground into flour, whilst almond flour is blanched (skin removed) and ground into a flour.

Because almond flour is higher in fat and protein than all-purpose flour, it's not the best substitute when making a loaf of bread or anything cake-like that does NOT call for eggs. Don't substitute almond flour for other flours unless the method says so!

Nut flours are more expensive to purchase than whole nuts, so to save costs you could purchase your nut of choice (almonds, hazelnuts, peanuts, cashew) and pulse in a food processor until a flour consistency (but stop before it turns into nut butter).

OAT FLOUR: made from rolled oats, ground into a flour consistency using a food processor or powerful blender. Other flours that could be substituted are wholemeal spelt flour, white spelt flour, gluten-free flour or plain flour. I recommend processing a large amount at once to have on hand.

COCONUT FLOUR: a great gluten-free, low carb and keto friendly flour for breads and baked goods. It contains protein and fewer digestible (net) carbs than any other flour, and even has fewer digestible carbs than most vegetables. Cannot be substituted for other flours in recipes, as it is highly absorbent and generally needs a lot of liquid in recipes.

VEGAN EGGS: chia seeds and ground flaxseed are an excellent source of healthy fats and some protein. They also make a great plantbased substitute for eggs! You make them by simply soaking 1 tbsp of chia seeds/ground flaxseed in 3 tbsp of water for 5 minutes until thickened. You can keep in the fridge for 2-3 days prior to use in baking.

NUTS & SEEDS: It's great to have a variety of nuts and seeds on hand, as they're super versatile in recipes, adding taste, texture and nutrition in the form of plantbased protein and healthy fats.

HEMP SEEDS: Also known as hemp hearts, hemp has one of the highest levels of protein of any plant and is an incredible and sustainable source of important plant-based protein andcontains vital Amino Acids, Essential Fatty Acids and nutrients. These little green superfoods can reduce the risk of disease, improve heart and brain function, reduce inflammation and increase energy and immunity. They're my favourite way of adding protein to anything and everything, and in this book I'd add a teaspoon or two to smoothies, yoghurt, oatmeal or any recipe to boost this essential nutrient (even if it doesn't call for it!) They have a delicious nutty taste and are incredibly versatile.

My staple wholefoods

DATES: By adding sweetness with dates, you can tone down the amount of added sugar in the dish. Chopped dates can also be added in moderation to oatmeal, or yogurt in place of honey or maple syrup, while whole, pitted dates can be blended into a smoothie mix to sweeten it. Dates are a great source of various vitamins and minerals, energy, and fiber. It also contains calcium, iron, phosphorus, potassium, magnesium and zinc.

COCONUT SUGAR: Coconut sugar is also called coconut palm sugar. It's a natural sugar made from coconut palm sap, which is the sugary circulating fluid of the coconut plant. The subtly sweet taste is similar to brown sugar with a hint of caramel. Unrefined and unprocessed, it is considered to be the healthier option compared to other refined and chemical sweetener options. It is important to note that it is not a nutritional superfood, it contains calories like normal sugars.

XYLITOL: Xylitol is a sugar-free sweetener that looks and tastes like sugar but has fewer calories and doesn't raise blood sugar levels. It is produced by extracting the all-natural sugar alcohol contained in the bark of birch trees. Generally, you can replace your sugar with a 1:1 ratio of xylitol.

HONEY & MAPLE SYRUP: Liquid sweeteners that can be used interchangeably.

FRESH FRUIT: is also a natural sweetener! Bananas and apple puree not only sweeten but are great for binding recipes aswell.

ALMOND MILK: is my preferred plantbased milk of choice for it's taste, texture and health benefits. Canned coconut milk and coconut cream are also great for creamier, thicker textures.

RAW CACAO POWDER & COCOA POWDER:
Unlike traditionally processed cocoa powder, which is heavily processed, raw cacao is the unprocessed version of the cacao bean. Raw cacao has far superior nutritional qualities to cocoa or chocolate, and a delicious and decadent chocolate flavour. Cacao is very nutrient dense, high in antioxidants as well as nutrients like magnesium (which can help reduce stress), potassium, and iron. It is referred to simply as 'cacao powder' in this book. You can also use cocoa powder as a substitute for cacao powder, however it has less benefits, but it has a more traditional "chocolate" taste.

SUGAR-FREE CHOCOLATE: Dark chocolate is rich in antioxidants, and all flavours of chocolate are guaranteed to be good for your soul! I use Well Naturally Sugar-Free Chocolate which has a high percentage of cocoa, is naturally gluten-free and sweetened with stevia. I gently melt it down in a bain marie and pipe it into chocolate chip shapes, for any recipe that requires chocolate chips.

EXTRA VIRGIN OLIVE OIL: Any recipe in this book that references olive oil is referring to high quality, extra virgin olive oil, and it can be used wherever oil is called for in the book. Extra virgin olive oil is perfectly safe to cook with, it stands up well to heat due to its monunsaturated fatty acid and phenolic compounds content and fares much better than other vegetable oils. It's full of healthy fats, antioxidants and is super satisfying. It's a great oil to eat both in taste and health and shouldn't be avoided. I use Light Flavour Extra Virgin Olive Oil from Cobram Estate, which was named the World's Healthiest Extra Virgin Olive Oil. It is a subtle blend with beautiful ripe fruit and apple notes with a distinct sweetness in the palate. The perfect choice when you want the food to tell the story!

COCONUT OIL: Coconut oil is another oil that's high in healthy saturated fats that have different effects than most other fats in your diet. These fats can boost metabolism and provide your body and brain with quick energy. They also raise the good HDL cholesterol in your blood, which is linked to reduced heart disease risk. Not to mention, it tastes delicious! Most recipes require coconut oil to be gently melted as unlike olive oil, it is solid at room temperature.

RECOMMENDED BRANDS

These are the brands I've loved and used for years, in sustainable cooking and cleaning. I cannot recommend these brands enough and I vouch for their success in Nourish In 5 recipes!

Many pantry staples are from Organic Road and Natural Road brands from Go Vita, a leading Australian Health Food Store.

 Well Naturally is my favourite sugar-free chocolate (that does NOT taste sugar-free!) It has a velvety taste and texture that I haven't been able to find in any other sugar-free chocolate brand.

 Cobram Estate olive oil is the highest quality olive oil on the market, and can be used in any recipe that calls for oil.

 13 Seeds is my hemp brand of choice, their high quality hemp protein, hemp flour, and hemp hearts (called hemp seeds in this book) are grown in Tasmania and family-run.

 Corn Thins are made from delicious popped corn and thin on calories, not on taste. In this book, I recommend using Corn Thins Wholegrain and Ancient Grains to add nutritious crunch to the recipe, but any of their range will work.

 ENJO Australia quite literally cleans the world, and I have a lot of respect and gratitude for this 25 year old, eco-friendly cleaning brand. Like the brand values of this book, they believe in putting healthy living first, and look to challenge the conventional and shine a light on sustainable living with a range of safe and effective fibre cleaning products that need absolutely no chemicals. I use their Kitchen Bundle range for all my kitchen and household cleaning needs.

Break-
fast

You Nutter!

Nutter Butter Granola

VEGAN | NUT-FREE OPTIONS | DAIRY-FREE | OIL-FREE | 12 SERVINGS

You can truly make this Granola your own, this base recipe encourages you to go wild thinking of creative mix-ins!

INGREDIENTS

1/4 cup (60g) smooth nut or seed butter *(ensure it's runny, add 1/4 tsp of salt if unsalted)*
(Organic Road)

1/4 cup (85g) maple syrup
(Organic Road)

1 1/4 cups (150g) nuts or seeds of choice *(I use walnuts)*
(Organic Road)

1 cup (100g) rolled oats
(Organic Road)

Optional mix-ins: banana chips, choc chips - I call this combo Chunky Monkey

NUTRITIONAL INFO

126 CALORIES / 4G PROTEIN / 15G CARBS / 7G FAT / 1G DIETARY FIBRE PER SERVE

METHOD

1. Preheat oven to 160°C/325°F. Line a large baking tray with a reusable baking mat. Set aside.

2. Add nut/seed butter and maple syrup to a medium bowl. Whisk until very well incorporated and smooth.

3. Add nuts/seeds and oats. Using a rubber spatula, stir and fold until well combined.

4. Pour onto the prepared baking tray. Using the spatula, gently nudge granola into an even layer. Separate granola to create small clusters. Make space between clusters to allow for air to flow through and crisp up the granola.

5. Bake for 20 minutes. Using a heatproof spatula, gently flip granola, making sure to keep clusters intact. Bake for an additional 5-10 minutes, until edges are a deep golden brown and granola is just slightly soft. Granola will crisp up while cooling, about 30 minutes. Stir in any optional mix-ins. Store in an airtight container at room temperature for 1 month, or freezer for 3 months.

Fluffy Vegan Vanilla Waffles

VEGAN | FLOURLESS | SUGAR-FREE | MAKES 8 WAFFLES

The best vegan waffle you'll ever have - golden, crispy, fluffy, full of flavor (especially with those gorgeous vanilla bean flecks). Plus, only 5 ingredients and 1 bowl! You can watch a video version of this on my YouTube channel, just search 'Amy Lee Active'.

INGREDIENTS

Waffles

1 1/2 cups *(about 3/4 of the can / 320g)* **full-fat coconut milk or coconut cream** *(Organic Road)*

1 vanilla bean, pods scraped out or 2 tsp vanilla extract

1 1/2 cups (225g) **oat flour** *(all-purpose, wholemeal spelt flour, gluten-free flour work) (Organic Road)*

1/3 cup (40g) **xylitol or coconut sugar** *(Organic Road)*

2 tsp baking powder

1/4 tsp salt *(Natural Road)*

Optional Toppings

Pure maple syrup

Butter or vegan butter

Fresh berries

NUTRITIONAL INFO

135G CALORIES / 1.8G PROTEIN / 8.4G CARBS / 11.1G FAT / 1.6G DIETARY FIBRE PER WAFFLE

METHOD

1. Preheat your non-stick waffle maker and grease if necessary.

2. If the coconut milk is solidified, gently heat in the microwave until liquid but not warm. Stir in the vanilla.

3. Sift in the flour, sweetener, baking powder, and salt. Stir in liquid until just combined (if you overmix, you risk making the waffles tough). Scoop batter into your waffle maker according to manufacturer instructions, as waffle makers vary. I add two tablespoons of batter per side in my waffle-maker. Cook for about 5-10 minutes or until golden brown.

4. Serve fresh with toppings of choice. Freeze for up to 1 month and just pop it in the toaster or oven to serve like fresh again.

NOTES

Other nut milks will work, it will just not be as rich-tasting.

Cacao Pops

VEGAN | MAKES 4 SERVES

I lived off Coco Pops as a kid, unknowingly consuming a sugary snack, not a nutritious breakfast cereal. I wanted to transform the fat and sugar-laden commercial version into a healthier, nutrient-dense (but still tasty!) version.

INGREDIENTS

3 tbsp (30g) coconut oil
(Organic Road)

3 tbsp (30g) raw cacao powder
(Organic Road)

3 tbsp (30g) maple syrup or honey if not vegan *(Organic Road)*

2 tbsp water

4 cups (96g) corn thins, crushed with hands *(I use Corn Thins Wholegrain)*

1 tbsp hemp protein powder
(13 Seeds)

NUTRITIONAL INFO

228 CALORIES / 4G PROTEIN / 32G CARBS / 9G FAT / 4G DIETARY FIBRE PER SERVE

METHOD

1. Preheat your oven to 160°C/320°F fan-forced.

2. In a small pot over low heat stir together coconut oil, cacao powder, maple syrup and water very gently, just until the coconut oil has melted. Taste and adjust, you may prefer it sweeter.

3. Add the puffed brown rice to a large mixing bowl, pour over the cacao mixture and stir gently until all the rice is well coated.

4. Transfer the chocolatey rice, spread apart as much as possible to two lined baking trays and bake for 10 minutes. Remove from the oven, immediately stir gently with a spoon so that the rice doesn't stick together, and leave to cool before transferring to a large glass jar for storage. Keeps for up to 1 month, and delicious served with a sliced banana and cold milk for breakfast!

Berry nice

Blueberry Pie Pancakes

VEGAN | FAT-FREE OPTION | SERVES 2-3 PEOPLE

The versatile pancake is not only light and fluffy, it's a delicious way to get a variety of fruits into your diet. Try these sweet pancakes drizzled with blueberries for a breakfast treat the whole family will love.

INGREDIENTS

1/3 cup oat flour (40g) + 2 tbsp rolled oats for texture (10g)

1 tbsp coconut sugar or xylitol for sugar-free *(Organic Road)*

1/2 tsp cinnamon *(Organic Road)*

2/3 tsp baking powder

1/8 tsp salt *(Natural Road)*

1 tbsp (10g) olive oil*

1/4 cup (60g) milk of choice

1/2 tsp vanilla extract

1/2 cup fresh or frozen blueberries

NUTRITIONAL INFO

189 CALORIES / 2G PROTEIN / 31G CARBS / 5G FAT / 3G DIETARY FIBRE PER SERVE OUT OF 3 SERVINGS

METHOD

1. Combine dry ingredients in a bowl, then add wet, (except blueberries) until just combined. Mix, but don't overmix. Gently stir through blueberries.

2. Drop a heaping tablespoon of batter on a lightly greased non-stick pan on low-medium, flipping each pancake once. Top with syrup, powdered sugar, or coconut whipped cream on page 232 . Or you could even boil some more blueberries (with a bit of coconut sugar or xylitol, if you wish), and smash them, to make a compote.

TIPS

*You can reduce the fat content by replacing the oil with apple puree.

VETO Bircher 3 Ways

VEGAN | KETO | MAKES 3 SERVES

This bircher is rich in healthy fats from plant-based sources, making it a super creamy, low-carb breakfast option.

INGREDIENTS

Bircher

2/3 cup (160g) almond or coconut milk

1/2 cup (75g) hemp seeds
(13 Seeds)

1 tbsp chia seeds

Optional: 1-2 tsp xylitol or sweeten with berries

1/2 tsp vanilla extract

Optional Toppings

Handful of nuts or seeds

Extra hemp seeds

Berries

NUTRITIONAL INFO

189 CALORIES / 9G PROTEIN / 3G CARBS / 16G FAT / 3G DIETARY FIBRE PER SERVE

METHOD

1. Stir all ingredients in a large bowl or container. Cover and refrigerate overnight or for 8 hours.

2. Stir again and divide into two bowls or containers. To serve, add toppings if desired. Store leftovers for 2-3 days in the fridge.

NOTES

• Sugar-free sweeteners are all different in terms of potency of sweetness compared to sugar.

• If using canned coconut milk, I mix 1 can of coconut milk with 1 can of filtered water then I shake and place into milk bottle in fridge. This is a much more economical way of utilising coconut milk as canned coconut milk tends to be thicker than other plant milks. You can also do this with coconut cream, adding 2-4 cans filled with water. Always try to buy coconut milk that doesn't contain added ingredients. Look for: coconut flesh, guar gum and water only.

VETO = Vegan Keto

VARIATIONS

- **VETO Fudge Bircher #2** In addition to the ingredients above, add 2 tablespoons of cacao powder and 1 tablespoon of almond butter or sunflower butter. Follow the same method as above. Optional toppings include shredded unsweetened coconut, cacao nibs, and berries.

- **VETO Pumpkin Spice Latte Bircher #3** Omit 1/3 cup (80 ml) of the coconut milk from the above base recipe, and replace with 1/3 cup (80 ml) brewed coffee. In addition to the ingredients above, add 2 tablespoons of canned pumpkin puree, and 3/4 teaspoon pumpkin pie spice (or 1/2 teaspoon ground cinnamon, 1/4 teaspoon ground nutmeg, and 1/8 teaspoon ground cloves). Follow the same method as above. Optional toppings include pecans, and ground cinnamon.

Hemp Protein Pancakes

PALEO | HIGH PROTEIN | MAKES 8 MEDIUM PANCAKES

Adding hemp protein is my favourite way of boosting my intake of essential amino acids! It's a natural, plant-based source of complete protein that also packs in antioxidants, minerals, fiber and heart-healthy unsaturated fats.

INGREDIENTS

1 banana

2 eggs

1/2 cup (50g) almond flour

2 tbsp (20g) hemp protein powder *(13 Seeds)*

1/2 tsp vanilla extract

2 tsp baking powder *(optional, but helps it rise)*

1/4 tsp cinnamon *(Organic Road)*

Pinch of salt *(Natural Road)*

OPTIONAL TO SERVE

Nut butter

Berries

Maple syrup

NUTRITIONAL INFO

74 CALORIES / 5G PROTEIN / 6G CARBS / 4G FAT / 2G DIETARY FIBRE PER SERVE

METHOD

1. Add all of the pancake ingredients to a food processor or blender and blend until smooth.

2. Thin the batter out with a little bit of your favorite milk, if needed.

3. Add a little bit of oil to a pan (I use a cast iron) over medium heat. Pour pancakes using a ¼ cup measuring cup and allow to cook until bubbles start to form.

4. Flip the pancakes and continue cooking for another 1–3 minutes until ready.

5. Serve with toppings of choice and enjoy!

Get hemp healthy!

Strawberry Shortcake Pancakes

PALEO | LOW CARB | MAKES 6 LARGE PANCAKES

Satisfy your berry dessert cravings with these Strawberry Shortcake Pancakes! They're a hit with anyone, especially served with Strawberry Soft Serve on top (recipe on the same page)

INGREDIENTS

1 cup (100g) almond flour

1/4 cup (24g) coconut flour
(Organic Road)

2-3 tbsp (17g) coconut sugar for Paleo option or xylitol for **sugar-free** *(Organic Road)*

1 tsp baking powder

2 eggs + 3 egg whites (90g)

1/4 cup (60g) olive oil, melted
(Cobram Estate)

1/3 cup water (85g)

1 1/2 tsp vanilla extract

METHOD

1. Whisk all dry ingredients together in a bowl. Stir in all wet ingredients until it forms a pancake batter. If it's too thick, add a little more milk or water.

2. Preheat a non-stick pan over medium heat. Pour the batter onto the pan in circle shape. Cover and cook about 1-2 mins until bubbles start to form. Flip and cook another minute or until golden brown on the other side. Repeat with the rest of the batter. Serve with Strawberry Soft Serve, fresh strawberries and coconut on top.

NUTRITIONAL INFO

267 CALORIES / 9G PROTEIN / 10G CARBS / 19G FAT / 5G DIETARY FIBRE PER SERVE

Strawberry Soft Serve

INGREDIENTS

3 strawberries

1 frozen banana

METHOD

1. Bliz it all together in a food processor until creamy.

2. Dollop onto your pancakes and enjoy!

Overnight Oats 5 Ways

VEGAN | MAKES 3 SERVES

A quick and simple breakfast or snack that you can prepare the night before! It's ideal for those who struggle to get out of bed (me) or who don't have time in the morning.

Pop the oats in a lidded jar for on-the-go convenience.

The hemp seeds add protein and make the oats super creamy, without having to use a stove like traditional porridge.

INGREDIENTS

1 1/2 cups (360g) almond milk

1 cup (100g) rolled oats

3 tbsp (30g) hemp seeds

1 medium banana mashed (about 120g) or apple puree

1/2 tsp cinnamon

METHOD

1. The night before, stir together all ingredients in a sealed container or bowl. Store in the fridge overnight. The next morning, mix the oats again to ensure everything Is evenly distributed.

2. Optional to add the mix-ins listed below.

NUTRITIONAL INFO

240 CALORIES / 9G PROTEIN / 33G CARBS / 9G FAT / 6G DIETARY FIBRE PER SERVE

Mocha
- 1/4 cup brewed coffee, room temperature or chilled
- 3 tsp mini chocolate chips, for topping

Apple Pie
- 1 medium apple (180g), chopped and stewed

Carrot Cake
- 1/2 cup carrot, finely grated
- 1/4 cup peacans or walnuts, chopped
- 3 tbsp raisins
- 1/4 tsp all spice

Peanut Butter & Jam
- 1/4 cup (145g) peanut butter
- 1/2 cup berry chia jam

For those who like sleep-ins!

Blueberry & Banana Bread
- 1 cup (145g) fresh blueberries

53

Coconut Crêpes

PALEO | GLUTEN-FREE | MAKES 6 LARGE CRÉPES

*All the deliciousness of the famous French thin pancakes,
but with all natural ingredients.*

INGREDIENTS

1/2 cup (60g) coconut flour
(Organic Road)

1/2 cup (60g) arrowroot flour

6 eggs

1 1/5 cups (360g) almond milk

Optional: 2 tbsp coconut sugar
for Paleo or xylitol for sugar-free
*(I prefer to sweeten with fruit on
top) (Organic Road)*

TOPPINGS

Coconut yoghurt, berries,
pomegranate seeds, chopped nuts

NUTRITIONAL INFO

205 CALORIES / 11G PROTEIN
/ 17G CARBS / 9G FAT / 10G
DIETARY FIBRE PER SERVE

METHOD

1. Whisk together the coconut flour,
   arrowroot and sweetener in a medium
   bowl.

2. In a separate bowl, whisk the eggs and
   milk until well combined. Pour wet into
   dry, whisking until smooth. Cover and
   refrigerate for 15 minutes to let the coconut
   flour soak.

3. Heat a non-stick skillet over medium heat,
   optional to lightly grease with oil. Pour a
   quarter cup of batter into the pan and
   gently swirl to coat pan in an even layer.
   Cook for about 1 minute until the surface
   dries out and the underside is golden. Flip
   and cook for another 30-45 seconds, or
   until golden. Transfer to a plate, cover to
   keep warm and set aside. Repeat.

4. Serve with optional toppings. Batter can
   be kept for up to 5 days refrigerated in a
   sealed container. Cooked crêpes can be
   kept for 5 days in the fridge and frozen for
   up to 3 months.

Wholemeal Scrolls

VEGAN | MAKES 10 SCROLLS

There's nothing better than freshly baked scrolls straight from the oven, especially when they contain wholesome, plantbased ingredients. It's also a great start to the day, containing slow release carbs and protein to keep you nourished for hours.

INGREDIENTS

Scroll

1 cup (90g) rolled oats
(Organic Road)

2 cups (300g) wholemeal spelt flour *(Organic Road)*

2 1/2 tsp baking powder

1/4 cup (55g) coconut oil
(Organic Road)

1 cup (250ml) almond milk

2 tsp apple cider vinegar
(Organic Road)

Filling

1/4 cup (50g) coconut sugar or xylitol for sugar-free
(Organic Road)

1/2 cup (115g) butter/vegan butter, melted or apple puree for low fat

1 1/2 tbsp cinnamon
(Organic Road)

Optional: 1/2 cup raisins or chopped pecans, + extra for topping

NUTRITIONAL INFO

233 CALORIES / 3.5G PROTEIN / 28.6G CARBS / 11.7G FAT / 3.3G DIETARY FIBRE PER SERVE

METHOD

1. **SCROLL:** Lightly grease a 20cm round cake pan.

2. Process oats in the food processor until a finely milled flour consistency. Process wholemeal spelt flour and baking powder until combined. Add coconut oil and blend until mixture resembles breadcrumbs.

3. Stir through almond milk and vinegar, and knead until a dough forms on a surface lightly dusted with flour. Roll dough out onto reusable baking mat, until it is a rectangle shape, about 20cm x 35cm.

4. Filling: Stir together all filling ingredients, pour all over dough and spread evenly over the surface with the back of a spoon. Refrigerate dough for 20 minutes or until chilled.

5. Preheat oven to 180°C/360°F fan-forced. Roll dough up firmly, starting from the long side. Cut roll into 10 x 3.5cm thick slices. Place scrolls cut side up in the pan, starting from the middle and working your way outwards, it's ok if the scrolls touch. Optional to scatter the top of the scrolls with raisins or pecans. Bake for 40 minutes or until a skewer inserted into the centre comes out clean (cover with foil if over-browning). Stand for 5 minutes before serving. Optional to make drizzle Coconut "Buttercream" on top (page 233).

what dreams are made of

Healthy Pop Tarts

SUGAR-FREE | DAIRY-FREE | LOW FAT | MAKES 10 POP TARTS

Yes, healthy pop tarts. Pop tarts without the corn syrup. Without the food dyes, without the trans fats. Healthy pop tarts with real fruit, with whole grains, with ingredients you can pronounce. And best of all, you won't miss the real thing with this delicious recipe!

INGREDIENTS

1/2 cup (75g) wholemeal spelt flour *(Organic Road)*

1 1/2 cup (150g) almond flour *(Organic Road)*

1/4 cup (55g) xylitol *(Organic Road)*

1/4 cup (60g) cold almond milk

1 egg yolk

2 tsp vanilla extract

Filling

1/2 cup Berry Chia Jam on page 228

NUTRITIONAL INFO

63 CALORIES / 2.1G PROTEIN / 8.3G CARBS / 2.8G FAT / 1.2G DIETARY FIBRE PER SERVE

METHOD

1. Sift spelt flour, almond flour and xylitol in a bowl, whisk to combine. Stir together egg yolk, almond milk and vanilla, until ingredients just come together into a pastry dough. Place dough in bowl, cover with beeswax wrap (reusable glad wrap) and refrigerate for 30 minutes. Make Berry Chia Jam if not already prepared.

2. Preheat oven to 160°C/320°F fan-forced. Divide pastry in equal halves, roll each portion between sheets of baking paper until 5mm thick, then slice the dough into 20 squares (to make 10 pop tarts). Place squares on reusable baking mat on a baking tray. Top each square with 1 tsp of jam, then place another square pastry on top, pressing edges gently to seal. Using a fork, press edges of pop tarts to create a pattern, and poke a hole on top to let air circulate. Brush tops with egg white for shine.

3. Bake pop tarts for 20 minutes until golden brown. Best eaten on the day, or let cool then store in refrigerator for about 3 days, or freeze for up to one month. To reheat, pop back into the oven for 10 minutes at 180°C/360°F fan-forced.

Cult
Cookies

Chocolate Cookie Sandwiches with Peanut Butter Cookie Dough

PROTEIN | VEGAN | MAKES 8 COOKIE SANDWICHES/16 COOKIES

Make these scrumptious Cookie Sandwiches filled with Peanut Butter Cookie Dough for your post-workout healthy snack, you won't regret it! An incredibly satisfying plantbased snack with 14g of protein per cookie sandwich!

INGREDIENTS

Chocolate Cookies

1 can (just under 2 cups) black beans, drained and well-rinsed

1/2 cup (120g) *peanut butter or almond butter (add 1/4 tsp salt if unsalted) *(Natural Road)*

1/4 cup water

1/4 cup (30g) cocoa powder *(Organic Road)*

1/4 cup (60g) coconut sugar *(Organic Road)*

1 tsp baking powder

1/2 cup (45g) vegan chocolate chips

Peanut Butter Cookie Dough

1/3 cup (85g) peanut butter (add 1/4 tsp salt is unsalted)

3 tbsp maple syrup *(Organic Road)*

1/2 cup (60g) water

3/4 cup (70g) coconut flour *(Organic Road)*

2 scoops (60g) protein powder *(Natural Road)*

1/4 cup (45g) vegan chocolate chips

METHOD

1. **CHOCOLATE COOKIES:** Preheat oven to 175°C/350°F fan-forced.

2. Add the first 3 ingredients to a food processor and mix until smooth. Add the cocoa powder, coconut sugar and baking powder and mix until smooth. Stir through the chocolate chips or pulse quickly in food processor.

3. Drop a heaped tablespoons of the batter onto a lined baking tray to form 16 cookies. The batter will seem quite wet but that's normal. Spread each out around slightly as they won't spread during baking. Bake for 17 minutes, remove and let cool on the pan completely before handling. They will seem under done when you take them out but will firm as they cool.

4. **COOKIE DOUGH:** Warm the peanut butter, maple syrup and water and stir in a bowl. Sift in coconut flour and protein powder, stir to combine. Stir through chocolate chios

5. **ASSEMBLY:** Scoop a ball of dough and flatten between two cookies to form a cookie sandwich. Store in fridge in an airtight container for up to 5 days.

TIPS

*Make sure you use runny nut butter or sunflower seed butter, I use Organic Road brand from Go Vita. Also works with whey

You can eat the dough or the cookies on their own if you don't want to make cookie sandwiches!

NUTRITIONAL INFO

CHOCOLATE COOKIES: 79 CALORIES / 2.4G PROTEIN / 8.4G CARBS /
4.9G FAT / 1.3G DIETARY FIBRE PER COOKIE OUT OF 16 COOKIES

PEANUT BUTTER COOKIE DOUGH: 191 CALORIES / 9.3G PROTEIN / 19.9G
CARBS / 9.5G FAT / 5.7G DIETARY FIBRE PER SERVE OUT OF 8 SERVES

Crunchy Choc Chip Cookies

VEGAN | MAKES 16 COOKIES

I always thought I was a soft cookie person...until I made these Crunchy Choc Chip Cookies. These will change your whole perspective on cookies; you won't believe they're made from wholesome ingredients!

INGREDIENTS

1 cup (150g) self-raising flour*
(if not self-raising, add 1/2 tsp baking soda)

1/2 cup (80g) coconut sugar
(Organic Road)

1/4 tsp salt *(Natural Road)*

2 1/2 tbsp almond milk

3 tbsp (36g) oil
(Organic Road Coconut Oil or Cobram Estate Olive Oil)

1/4 tsp vanilla extract

1/4 cup (45g) mini sugar-free choc chips** *(Well Naturally)*

NUTRITIONAL INFO

96 CALORIES / 1G PROTEIN / 15G CARBS / 4G FAT / 1G DIETARY FIBRE PER COOKIE

METHOD

1. Preheat oven to 150°C/300°F fan-forced. Line a baking tray with a non-stick baking mat.

2. Combine first 5 ingredients in a large bowl. Stir in remaining ingredients to form a dough – it will be very dry at first, so keep stirring and breaking up clumps until it turns into cookie dough. You should not need more liquid.

3. Roll dough into 16 balls. Place on the prepared tray, then press down to flatten. They expand a lot as they cook, so leave room between cookies. Bake for 15 minutes, then let cool for 10 minutes before removing from the tray. They become crispier as they cool. Crispy cookies are best stored in a glass jar/container instead of plastic.

TIPS

Spelt or oat flour also work, but the result is not as crispy. Oat flour is made from rolled oats processed into a flour consistency. I use Organic Road Rolled Oats.

**I make the mini choc chips myself by melting Well Naturally sugar-free chocolate and piping small dots of chocolate onto a non-stick baking mat.

Nutter Butter Cookies

VEGAN | PALEO | GLUTEN-FREE | MAKES 12 COOKIES

You can use any nut or seed butter that your heart desires. These are a crowd-pleaser, your friends and family will be shocked that these cookies are vegan as they're packed full of nutty, buttery flavour.

INGREDIENTS

1 cup nut or seed butter*
(I recommend almond butter)
(Organic Road)

**3/4 cup coconut sugar or xylitol
for sugar-free** *(Organic Road)*

1 flax egg** or egg if not vegan**
(Organic Road)

1/4 tsp baking soda

1/4 tsp salt *(Natural Road)*

NUTRITIONAL INFO

96 CALORIES / 1G PROTEIN /
15G CARBS / 4G FAT / 1G
DIETARY FIBRE PER COOKIE

METHOD

1. Preheat the oven to 175ºC/350ºF fan-forced and line a baking tray.

2. In a large bowl, stir together the almond butter, coconut sugar, egg, baking soda, and salt until it is a thick, uniform batter.

3. Use an ice cream scoop to scoop dough onto the baking tray, keeping the cookies spaced apart. Flatten and use a fork to form a pattern if desired. Bake the cookies until lightly golden, about 12 to 13 minutes. For a crispier cookie, you can bake them for 15-20 minutes, just watch to make sure that they don't burn.

4. Allow the cookies to cool completely before serving. They are fragile when warm, and firm up when cool. You can store the cookies in an airtight container unrefrigerated for a couple days, but store them in the fridge or freezer for a longer shelf life. (They are extra-crunchy served frozen.)

NOTES

*You can use any nut or seed butter for these cookies.. Note that if you use sunflower seed butter, the inside of the cookies may turn green due to a safe chemical reaction that happens with the baking soda.

**To make one flax egg, soak one tablespoon of ground flaxseed in three tablespoons of water, let soak for 5 minutes. *(I use Organic Road ground flaxseed).*

and piping small dots of chocolate onto a non-stick baking mat.

A crowd-pleaser

I've fallen in love xx

Chocolate Salted Caramel Thumbprint Cookies

VEGAN | PALEO | GLUTEN-FREE | MAKES 10

You're going to fall in love with these buttery, chocolatey cookies - you won't believe they're plantbased and full of antioxidants.

INGREDIENTS

2 cups (200g) almond flour

1/4 cup (30g) cacao or cocoa powder *(Organic Road)*

1/3 cup (65g) coconut sugar (xylitol for sugar-free) *(Organic Road)*

6 tbsp (85g) vegan butter, soft

3/4 cup vegan caramel sauce *(page 236, or store-bought)*

NUTRITIONAL INFO

159 CALORIES / 3.7G PROTEIN / 11.9G CARBS / 11.6G FAT / 2.3G DIETARY FIBRE PER COOKIE

METHOD

1. Preheat oven to 175°C/350°F fan-forced. Prepare a baking tray with a non-stick baking mat.

2. In a bowl, stir together the almond flour, cocoa powder and sugar. Mix in the softened butter until a dough forms.

3. Use an ice cream scoop to form 10 evenly sized balls. Place the balls spread apart on the baking tray, flatten gently with the back of your hand, then make an indent in the middle with your thumb. Bake for 6-8 minutes. They will be soft when you remove them but will firm up into a fudgy texture as they cool. Once completely cool, fill cookies with caramel and serve. Cookies are best if stored in an airtight container in the refrigerator.

TIPS

Try filling with berry chia jam (page 228) for a choc berry flavour!

Paleo Choc Chip Cookies

PALEO | VEGAN | GLUTEN-FREE | MAKES 10 LARGE COOKIES

The perfect soft cookie full of natural,
wholesome ingredients.

INGREDIENTS

2 cups (200g) almond flour

1/4 tsp salt *(Natural Road)*

1/4 cup (60g) almond butter
(Organic Road)

1/4 cup (25g) coconut oil
(Organic Road)

1/4 cup (85g) honey or maple syrup *(Organic Road)*

1/2 cup (75g) sugar-free dark chocolate chips *(Well Naturally)*

NUTRITIONAL INFO

206 CALORIES / 6G PROTEIN /17 G CARBS / 14G FAT / 3G DIETARY FIBRE PER SERVE

METHOD

1. Preheat oven to 175°C/350°F.

2. In a bowl, add almond flour, chocolate chips, and sea salt.

3. In a small, microwave safe bowl, add almond butter, coconut oil, and honey. Microwave in 15-20 second intervals until mixture is warmed and liquid but not hot. Mix together well.

4. Pour wet mixture over the almond flour mixture, and mix well to combine.

5. Line a baking sheet with baking paper, and form small tablespoon sized balls of dough. Flatten into a cookie shape.

6. Bake for 8-11 minutes, until just starting to brown on top.

7. Allow to fully cool, and the cookies will firm up

You can't
beat a
Pb & j

No Bake Peanut Butter & Jelly Thumbprint Cookies

PROTEIN | VEGAN | GLUTEN-FREE | MAKES 12 COOKIES

You'll notice there are a lot of peanut butter and jelly combinations in this book, and that's because you really can't beat the flavour combination of nutty and fruity - you'll adore this no-bake, no-fuss cookie, with added natural protein from hemp seeds.

INGREDIENTS

COOKIES

1/2 cup (120g) peanut butter
(or sub other nut/seed butter)
(add 1/4 tsp salt if unsalted)
(Organic Road)

1/4 cup (85g) liquid sweetener
(I recommend maple syrup)
(Organic Road)

1 1/3 cup (135g) almond flour*
(or half this amount in coconut flour, plus more as needed)

1/4 cup (30g) hemp seeds
(13 Seeds)

JAM

**1 cup store-bought jam
or berry chia jam (page 228)**

NUTRITIONAL INFO

151 CALORIES / 6G PROTEIN / 10G CARBS / 12G FAT / 2G DIETARY FIBRE PER SERVE

METHOD

1. Combine peanut butter and liquid sweetener in a bowl.

2. Measure out almond flour and add a little at a time until a workable dough forms. If too dry/crumbly, add more peanut butter or maple syrup. If too sticky or wet, add a little more almond flour.

3. Scoop dough using an ice cream scoop and roll into balls. Use your thumb to gently press a thumbprint into the cookie. If the dough cracks, smooth the cracks over before adding jam. Continue until all cookies are pressed.

4. Add 1/2 tsp of jam to the center of each cookie, repeat until all cookies are filled. Store cookies in an air-tight container in the refrigerator up to 1 week, or in the freezer up to 1 month (let thaw before enjoying).

TIPS

You can sub out 1/3 of the almond flour for protein powder of choice to make this even more protein-packed!

Peanut Butter Hemp Protein Cookies

PROTEIN | VEGAN | MAKES 12 COOKIES

A yummy peanut buttery cookie with all the goodness of hemp protein to keep you fuller for longer. This is a great cookie recipe for those who are beginners of cooking with hemp to cookies.

INGREDIENTS

2/3 cup (165g) peanut butter
(Organic Road)

2 eggs

1/3 cup (65g) coconut sugar
(Organic Road)

1/3 cup (45g) hemp seeds
(13 Seeds)

2/3 cup (90g) rolled oats
(Organic Road)

1 tsp vanilla extract

Optional: melted chocolate to decorate *(Well Naturally)*

NUTRITIONAL INFO

163 CALORIES / 6.7G PROTEIN / 13.6G CARBS / 10G FAT / 1.7G DIETARY FIBRE PER COOKIE

METHOD

1. Mix all the ingredients in a bowl.

2. Scoop onto a cookie sheet. (They stick a little so make sure you use a silpat, parchment paper or grease well)

3. Flatten with a fork and bake at 160°C375°F for 8–10 min. Let cool at least 5 min before removing from baking sheet.

ove you so matcha!

Matcha Oat Shortbread

VEGAN | PALEO | MAKES 12 COOKIES

I love adding matcha green tea powder to cookies, cakes, chocolate and more! It's full of antioxidants, rich in fiber, chlorophyll and vitamins, and can help boost your metabolism.

INGREDIENTS

1 cup (115g) oat flour*
(Organic Road)

1 tbsp (8g) matcha powder

1/4 tsp salt *(Natural Road)*

4 tbsp (30g) xylitol

1/4 c (25g) coconut oil, melted

2 tbsp milk of choice

Optional: pipe coconut cream on page 233 in between each cookie.

NUTRITIONAL INFO

WITH SKIM MILK: 99 CALORIES / 0G PROTEIN / 11G CARBS / 4G FAT / 0G DIETARY FIBRE PER SERVE

METHOD

1. Place the flour, matcha and salt into a bowl and stir until combined. Mix in coconut oil and in the milk and continue blending together until a dough forms. Wrap the dough in plastic and place in the freezer for 10 minutes.

2. Preheat oven to 175°C/350°F. Remove the dough from the freezer and kneed until the dough is soft like play dough. Place between two pieces of baking paper and roll out the dough until it's about 1/8 inch in thickness. Use a small cookie cutter (you could use the cap of your cinnamon spice) to make 12 cookies. These cookies will be fragile so the best way to do this is to cut out the cookies, remove the trim and let the cookie cutouts remain on the baking paper. Transfer the paper to a baking tray and bake for 8-10 minutes. Store in an airtight container at room temperature. Optional to pipe coconut cream in-between two cookies.

NOTES

Oat flour is rolled oats ground into flour consistency.protein powder of choice to make this even more protein-packed!

You'll Wanna Date Me Cookies

VEGAN | PALEO | MAKES 12 COOKIES

These cookies have the natural, caramelly sweetness of dates - they're so lovely, you'll probably want to DATE the person who makes them for you. They're the easiest, most deliciously chewy cookies made of just five natural ingredients. It's magic!

INGREDIENTS

1 3/4 cup (180g) almond meal or flour

12 medjool dates, pitted (about 250g)

1 tbsp chia seeds *(Organic Road)*

3 tbsp almond milk

Handful of raisins or sugar-free dark chocolate chips *(Well Naturally)*

NUTRITIONAL INFO

98 CALORIES / 1G PROTEIN / 19G CARBS / 3G FAT / 3G DIETARY FIBRE PER SERVE

METHOD

1. Preheat oven to 180°C/360°F fan-forced.

2. Process all of the ingredients (apart from your dark chocolate chips or raisins) in a food processor until it forms a dough. Add the dark chocolate chips or raisins and give it another very quick whizz to mix it all together.

3. Scoop a tablespoon of the mixture and roll them into balls and placing them on a lined baking sheet. Once you have about 12 round balls, squish them down to form cookie shapes. Bake in the oven for 15-20 minutes until golden. Store in an airtight container for up to 5 days.

It's magic baby

Almond Coco Shortbread

VEGAN | MAKES 16

This is going to be your staple vegan shortbread recipe.

INGREDIENTS

1/3 cup (80g) coconut butter, melted gently*

1/4 cup (80g) maple syrup
(Organic Road)

1/3 cup (40g) coconut flour
(Organic Road)

1 cup (100g) almond flour

Optional: 1 tsp almond extract

1/4 tsp salt

Optional: 1/2 cup (75g) sugar-free dark chocolate, melted
(Well Naturally)

NUTRITIONAL INFO

64 CALORIES / 1G PROTEIN / 6.2G CARBS / 4.2G FAT / 1.9G DIETARY FIBRE PER SERVE

METHOD

1. Preheat the oven to 175°C/350°F.

2. Whisk together the coconut butter, maple syrup, and almond extract if using.

3. Sift in the coconut flour, almond flour, and salt. Mix and knead to form a moist ball of dough.

4. Roll out to 1/4 inch thickness. Cut into circles (using a cookie cutter or a mason jar lid works too!) and transfer to a baking tray lined with a reusable baking mat.

5. Bake for 10 minutes or until golden around the edges. Remove from the oven and cool. They are delicious warm, but if you are going to dip them in chocolate, let them cool completely first. Keep leftovers in the refrigerator in an airtight container for up to a week.

NOTES

Coconut butter is best, but if you have to substitute use 1/3 cup runny cashew butter OR 1/4 cup coconut oil. I use Organic Road brand from Go Vita for all of these options.

Keto Burnt Butter Cookie Skillet

KETO | VEGAN | PALEO | MAKES 10 SLICES

This is the dessert to 'WOW' at parties and gatherings, and to shock and impress your friends when you tell them it's healthy!

INGREDIENTS

1/2 cup (115g) butter or vegan butter

1 large egg or flax egg
(Organic Road)

1 tsp vanilla extract

1/4 cup (35g) xylitol or coconut sugar if not strict KETO
(Organic Road)

2 cups almond flour (200g)
(You can substitute 1/2 cup of almond flour for 1/2 cup protein powder to boost the protein)

1/2 tsp salt *(Natural Road)*

1/2 cup (75g) sugar-free chocolate chips* *(Well Naturally)*

NUTRITIONAL INFO

177 CALORIES / 2.7G PROTEIN / 8.4G CARBS / 16.1G FAT / 1.4G DIETARY FIBRE PER SERVE

METHOD

1. Preheat oven to 175°C/350°F fan-forced. Heat the butter in a 9-inch non-stick pan over high heat until bubbling. Reduce heat and cover pan (optional; prevents butter spitting), and continue to cook, stirring occasionally until the butter starts to brown. Once browned, remove from heat and allow to cool for about 5 minutes.

2. While butter is cooling, whisk together the egg, vanilla and sweeteners in a bowl. Mix in the butter in the pan once it has cooled.

3. Sift in the almond flour into the bowl to remove lumps and add the salt and half the chocolate chips; mix through gently until the batter is well combined and creamy. It will be a little thicker than cookie dough. Smooth batter into skillet; top with remaining chocolate chips.

4. Bake for 20-25 minutes or until golden and firm on the top when pressed lightly and a toothpick inserted into the centre of the cookie comes out clean.Serve with sugar-free ice cream or frozen yogurt and enjoy!

TIPS

*I melt Well Naturally Sugar-Free Dark Chocolate and pipe into choc chip shapes.

Best of Both Worlds Cookie

VEGAN | PALEO | MAKES 12 COOKIES

This is the cookie for when you want the best of both worlds; chocolate AND peanut butter in a cookie.

INGREDIENTS

1 1/4 cup (145g) oat flour
(Organic Road)

1/2 cup (75g) coconut sugar
(Organic Road)

1/2 tsp baking powder

1/2 tsp salt *(Natural Road)*

3 tbsp (30g) olive oil
(I use Cobram Estate Olive Oil)

1/4 cup (65g) peanut butter

1 tbsp water

1 tsp vanilla extract

2 tbsp cocoa powder

Optional: 1/4 cup sugar-free chocolate chips *(Well Naturally)*

NUTRITIONAL INFO

156 CALORIES / 1.3G PROTEIN / 20.8G CARBS / 6.2G FAT / 0.7G DIETARY FIBRE PER SERVE

METHOD

1. Preheat oven to 175°C/350°F fan-forced. Line a tray with baking paper.

2. In a large mixing bowl, whisk together the oat flour, coconut sugar, protein powder, baking powder, and salt. Stir in the oil, peanut butter, vanilla extract.

3. Transfer half of the dough to another mixing bowl. Add the cocoa powder and 1 tbsp water. Mix until well combined. Stir in the chocolate chips if using. If the dough seems too dry, add one more teaspoon of water until you get the texture of a cookie dough.

4. Take about one and a half tablespoon of the chocolate cookie dough. Roll into a ball. Take one and a half tablespoon of the peanut butter cookie dough and roll it into a ball. Combine the two balls together to form one larger ball. Place it on the baking sheet and flatten with the palm of your hand, smooth the edges. You want to shape it into a cookie shape since it won't spread or flatten during baking. Repeat with the remaining dough.

5. Bake for 13-15 minutes, or until the edges appear golden brown. Remove from the oven and let cool completely on the baking sheet. Cookies will be soft at first but will firm up as they cool. Store in an airtight container, or wrap each cookie individually in plastic wrap. Cookies will keep for up to 2 weeks at room temperature.

Bars, Brownies & Breads

Coconut Choc Fudge Bars

VEGAN | NO-BAKE | SUGAR-FREE | MAKES 20 SMALL BARS

You won't believe how simple and effortless these decadent fudge bars are, I've never met anyone who didn't demolish the whole bar at once! You can also watch the recipe video of this on my YouTube channel (search "Amy Lee Active").

INGREDIENTS

3 cups (240g) shredded coconut
(Organic Road)

1/4 cup (30g) xylitol or coconut sugar if not sugar-free
(Organic Road)

1/2 cup coconut oil, melted (100g)
(Organic Road)

1 tsp vanilla extract

3/4 cup (130g) vegan or sugar-free chocolate chips, melted
(Well Naturally)

1/3 cup (85g) almond butter
(add 1/4 tsp salt if unsalted)
(Organic Road)

METHOD

1. Line an 8×8 baking pan. In a medium bowl, combine shredded coconut, xylitol, coconut oil and vanilla. Firmly press down 2/3 of the coconut mixture into the pan.

2. Stir together chocolate and almond butter to make the fudge, and evenly pour on top of the coconut layer. Sprinkle remaining coconut mixture on top, and refrigerate for 1 hour or until firm. Slice into bars. Store in fridge for a week, or freezer for 3 months.

NUTRITIONAL INFO

128 CALORIES / 1.3G PROTEIN / 5G CARBS / 12G FAT / 2.1G DIETARY FIBRE PER BAR

simple and effortless

89

Berrylicious Jam Crumble Bars

VEGAN | MAKES 12 BARS

This is THE dessert recipe to please anyone, especially if they don't believe that desserts made from healthy wholefoods can actually taste amazing. One of my absolute faves that I've made countless times for gatherings and parties.

INGREDIENTS

1 cup (250g) butter or vegan butter, cut into chunks

1 1/2 cup (225g) flour *(plain, wholemeal, spelt all work)*
(Organic Road)

3/4 cup (60g) rolled oats

3/4 cup (110g) coconut sugar or xylitol for sugar-free
(Organic Road)

1 1/2 cups berry chia jam
(page 228, or store-bought)

NUTRITIONAL INFO

USED STRAWBERRY JAM: 271 CALORIES / 2.8G PROTEIN / 26.9G CARBS / 14.7G FAT / 1G DIETARY FIBRE PER BAR

METHOD

1. Preheat oven to 190°C/375°F. Grease a brownie pan with oil/butter.

2. Measure all ingredients in separate bowls. In a food processor pulsate three quarters of the butter, flour, oats and sugar, reserving the other quarter of each ingredient for the topping. Pulsate until combined into a mealy mixture. Press into the prepared pan.

3. Spread the jam over the prepared layer. (If adding fruit - now is when you would add it)

4. In the food processor process the remaining ingredients for the topping until a crumbly mixture, then sprinkle over jam.

5. Bake for 25 minutes or until edges are golden brown, then remove from oven and allow to completely cool before cutting into squares (I cut big squares and got 32, but you could easily cut these into small squares for more!)

Peanut Butter Cup Protein Bars

HIGH PROTEIN | VEGAN | MAKES 12 BARS

Go nuts for this delicious protein bar that's inspired by peanut butter cups - only without the nasty palm oils and preservatives that the original contains! Include this tasty treat in your food prep for the week; it's the perfect protein packed gym snack.

INGREDIENTS

1 cup (220g) smooth peanut butter

1/4 cup (50g) liquid sweetener
(honey or maple syrup works best)
(Organic Road)

3 scoops (90g) vanilla protein powder*
(Natural Road)

1/2 cup (60g) oat flour
(Organic Road)

1/2 cup dark chocolate chips

NUTRITIONAL INFO

192 CALORIES / 11G PROTEIN / 14G CARBS / 11G FAT / 2G DIETARY FIBRE

METHOD

1. In a large bowl, whisk together the peanut butter and sweetener. Mix in the protein powder and oat flour until it becomes a dough.

2. Line an 8x8 inch baking pan with baking paper or glad wrap. Flatten batter into a pan evenly, so it fills the entire pan.

3. Place in freezer for 20 mins. Meanwhile, melt the chocolate in the microwave on low heat. Remove mixture from the freezer and cut into 12 bars.

4. Drizzle the melted chocolate over the bars and add chopped peanuts if desired. Store in an airtight container in the fridge, best enjoyed chilled.

TIPS

- *This can be made vegan, just use maple syrup and a vegan protein powder – different brands yield different results, so if it's too dry, add more liquid; if it's too wet, add more flour or protein powder.

- If you prefer, you roll them into protein balls, they hold their shape better out of the fridge!

Go nuts

Choc Chip Cookie Dough Protein Bars

HIGH PROTEIN | VEGAN | MAKES 10 BAR

Prep these bars for the week and you'll have a super satisfying, all-natural snack that will combat any 3pm sugar-cravings! Chickpeas are rich in protein, fibre, vitamins and minerals, giving the bar a naturally fudgy texture (and no, you can't taste them!) Everytime I serve these, people are always shocked that they contain legumes!

INGREDIENTS

1 can chickpeas*
(about 250g after draining)

2 tsp vanilla extract

1/4 tsp salt *(Natural Road)*

1/4 tsp baking soda

1/4 cup (55g) nut butter*
(Organic Road)

1/2 cup (50g) maple syrup or honey if not vegan *(Organic Road)*

1 1/2 cups (180g) rolled oats
(Organic Road)

1/3 cup (60g) vegan choc chips or sugar-free chocolate chips
(Well Naturally)

NUTRITIONAL INFO

233 CALORIES / 10G PROTEIN / 32G CARBS / 7G FAT / 7G DIETARY FIBRE PER BAR

METHOD

1. Process all ingredients except choc chips in a food processor until smooth. Stir through choc chips.

2. Spread the dough into an 8×8 lined pan, and freeze until firm for about half an hour.

3. Drizzle with melted chocolate, slice, and enjoy! These bars can be stored in the freezer for up to 3 months, just thaw before enjoying. Or they can keep in the fridge for 4-5 days. Optional to drizzle extra chocolate on top!

NOTES

*Any nut or seed butter will work.

Banana Bread Bars

VEGAN | MAKES 12 BARS

These banana bread bars are packed with nutrients with a dense and chewy texture - Since they don't have any flour or baking soda/powder, they don't rise and become fluffy. Because of this, they're super filling and a great balance of carbs, protein and fats. Perfect for packing into school or work lunchboxes.

INGREDIENTS

3 bananas, very ripe

1 cup (250g) peanut butter or almond butter *(Organic Road)*

1/4 cup (85g) maple syrup or honey if not vegan *(Organic Road)*

1 tsp cinnamon *(Organic Road)*

1 tsp vanilla extract optional

2 cups (200g) rolled oats
(Organic Road)

Optional: 1 cup sliced almonds or other nuts/seeds

NUTRITIONAL INFO

226 CALORIES / 4G PROTEIN / 34G CARBS / 8G FAT / 2G DIETARY FIBRE PER SERVE

METHOD

1. Preheat oven to 175°C/350°F. In a bowl, mix the first 5 ingredients until evenly combined.

2. Stir through the oats and almonds if using until combined.

3. Flatten mixture using a spatula onto lined 9x9 inch baking pan.

4. Bake for 30 minutes, or until golden brown on edges. Allow to cool completely before cutting bars. Store at room temperature for a week or freeze for up to 6 months in an airtight container or wrapped individually in plastic wrap.

TIPS

- Make it your own and add chocolate chips, other spices like nutmeg, or other extracts like almond.

- For a nut-free version, use sunflower seed butter instead of peanut butter and use sunflower seeds and/or pumpkin seeds instead of almonds.

- You can halve the recipe and use a loaf pan, bake for 20 mins and make 6 energy bars instead.

Perfect for work or school lunchboxes

Chocolate Peanut Butter Protein Crispy Bars

GLUTEN FREE | VEGAN | HIGH PROTEIN | MAKES 8 BARS

These grab-n-go bars are crunchy peanut butter perfection, with only a handful of ingredients you probably already have in your pantry. They'll be sure to satisfy your chocolate peanut butter cravings.

INGREDIENTS

CRISPY BARS

2 cups (48g) corn thins, crushed, about 8 rice cakes *(Corn Thins Wholegrain)*

1/2 cup (125g) peanut butter *(add 1/4 tsp salt if unsalted)*

1/3 cup (115g) maple syrup *(Organic Road)*

2 tbsp (20g) coconut oil *(Organic Road)*

2 tbsp (20g) protein powder *(13 Seeds Hemp Protein Powder)*

CHOCOLATE TOPPING

170g sugar-free dark chocolate, chopped *(Well Naturally)*

2 tbsp peanut butter

OPTIONAL GARNISH

¼ cup roasted peanuts, chopped

1 tsp flaky sea salt

NUTRITIONAL INFO

124 CALORIES / 6G PROTEIN / 16G CARBS / 6G FAT / 2G DIETARY FIBRE PER SERVE (NOT INCLUDING TOPPINGS)

METHOD

1. **BARS:** Line an 8x8" square baking pan with baking paper. Place the corn thins in a large bowl, crush into small pieces with your hands – don't use a food processor as it will turn into powder.

2. In a small saucepan, combine the peanut butter, maple syrup, coconut oil, and salt if using, over medium-low heat. Whisk to combine and bring to a boil. Turn down to a simmer and let bubble for 3 minutes, whisking the whole time. After 3 minutes, remove from the heat and pour over the corn thins. Stir to combine and coat completely.

3. Pour the mixture into the prepared pan and use a spatula to press the bars down firmly. Place in fridge to firm up.

4. **TOPPING:** chopped dark chocolate and peanut butter in a microwave safe bowl and microwave in 30 seconds increments, stirring between each, until it's smooth and melted.

5. Spread the chocolate over the peanut butter crispy bars. If using, garnish with peanuts and flaky sea salt.

6. Let firm up in the fridge for at least 30 minutes before cutting into 16 squares. Store in the refrigerator.

Banana Brownie Bites

VEGAN | MAKES 8

These ridiculously simple brownie bites are perfect for when you're craving a hit of chocolate combined with the sweetness of banana. They're loaded with fibre, potassium and nutrients.

INGREDIENTS

2 ripe bananas

1/2 cup (125g) nut butter
(I like almond butter, add 1/4 tsp of salt if unsalted) *(Organic Road)*

1/4 cup (30g) cacao powder
(Organic Road)

1/4 cup (85g) maple syrup
(Organic Road)

1 1/2 tbsp (12g) protein powder of choice *(Organic Road)*

METHOD

1. Preheat oven to 175ºC/350ºF fan-forced. Line an 8x8 baking tin.

2. In a bowl or food processor, mash the bananas, then mix in the rest of your ingredients.

3. Pour the batter in the prepared baking tin, smoothing evenly with a spatula. Bake for 22-25 minutes, until it's to the amount of done in the middle that you prefer. I baked for 22 minutes.

NUTRITIONAL INFO

140 CALORIES / 3G PROTEIN / 26G CARBS / 3G FAT / 2G DIETARY FIBRE PER SERVE

Decadence Brownies

GLUTEN-FREE OPTION | MAKES 15

These brownies live up to their name, they're super rich, fudgy and decadent, complete with the coveted crackly brownie top. Keep in mind that even though they are made from natural ingredients, they still have calories. These are the closest things to the naughty version, the ultimate decadence with natural ingredients.

INGREDIENTS

220g butter, melted *(coconut oil works, but not as rich-tasting)*

2 cups (200g) coconut sugar *(Organic Road)*

4 eggs

1 cup (150g) flour of choice *(plain, gluten-free, spelt, wholemeal) (Organic Road)*

2/3 cup (80g) cacao or cocoa powder *(Organic Road)*

1 tsp vanilla extract

1/4 tsp salt *(Natural Road)*

NUTRITIONAL INFO

234 CALORIES / 3G PROTEIN / 23G CARBS / 15G FAT / 2G DIETARY FIBRE PER SERVE

METHOD

1. Preheat oven to 175ºC/350ºF fan-forced. Line an 8x8 baking dish with baking paper.

2. Stir together the melted butter and sugar by hand or in a food processor. Stir in the eggs. Add the flour, cocoa powder, vanilla and salt and stir until you have a smooth batter.

3. Pour the batter into your baking dish and bake for 25–30 minutes. The top will look set, and a toothpick inserted will have moist crumbs on it, but it shouldn't have runny batter. Store brownies covered, at room temp for up to 3 days.

NOTES

If you want to serve these and have them hold their shape, you need to let them fully cool before cutting into them! If not, dig in!

Fresh & tangy

Easy Peasy Lemon Bars

SUGAR-FREE | MAKES 16 BARS

*Another tea party essential, these lemon bars
taste fresh and tangy without being super sweet.*

INGREDIENTS

SHORTBREAD CRUST

**1 1/2 cups (200g) flour of
choice** *(plain, spelt, wholemeal)*
(Organic Road)

3/4 cup (170g) cold butter, diced

**1/4 cup (35g) powdered
sweetener*** *(Organic Road)*

zest of 1 lemon

LEMON FILLING

4 large eggs

**1 cup (150g) powdered
sweetener*** *(Organic Road)*

**1/2 cup freshly-squeezed
lemon juice**

2 tbsp flour of choice

NUTRITIONAL INFO

175 CALORIES / 3G PROTEIN / 11G
CARBS / 10G FAT / 0G DIETARY
FIBRE PER SERVE

METHOD

1. Preheat oven to 175ºC/350ºF fan-forced. Line an 8 x 8-inch baking pan with baking paper.

2. **CRUST:** Combine all of the crust ingredients in a food processor. Pulse until the mixture reaches a fine crumble consistency. Press the mixture evenly into the prepared pan. Bake the crust for 20 minutes, or until it is lightly golden on top.

3. **FILLING:** Meanwhile, whisk the lemon filling ingredients together in a mixing bowl until combined. If there are lots of bubbles or clumps in the filling, pour the filling through a fine-mesh strainer to get it nice and smooth before adding it to the crust. (But if there are a few little clumps, that's ok too!)

4. **ASSEMBLY:** Once the crust is done baking, remove the pan from the oven and immediately pour the lemon filling on top of the hot crust. Return the pan to the oven and bake for 15-20 more minutes*, or until the lemon filling has set. Remove the pan from the oven and transfer to a wire baking rack to cool until the bars reach room temperature. Then transfer to the refrigerator and let the bars chill for at least 2 hours. Optional to sprinkle the tops of the bars with extra powdered sweetener, then slice and serve!

NOTES

*I process Organic Road Xylitol until it is in powdered form.

No-Bake Walnut Protein Brownies

GLUTEN-FREE | REFINED SUGAR-FREE | MAKES 12

This no bake healthy raw brownies recipe is so easy to make! It's the best raw brownie – gluten-free, no added sugar, and deliciously unbaked!

INGREDIENTS

1 cup (120g) dates, soaked for 10 minutes in boiling water, reserve date water

1/2 cup walnuts

1/2 cup protein powder of choice *(Natural Road)*

1 tbsp maple syrup *(Organic Road)*

1 tbsp cacao powder *(Organic Road)*

1/2 tsp cinnamon *(Organic Road)*

pinch of salt *(Natural Road)*

NUTRITIONAL INFO

103 CALORIES / 5G PROTEIN / 13.1G CARBS / 4.7G FAT / 2.4G DIETARY FIBRE PER SERVE

METHOD

1. Place the dates in a food processor or high speed blender and pulse a few times until broken down into pieces. Add remaining ingredients blend until evenly combined (but still some texture). It should be a little sticky when touched. If needed, add a little bit of date water to help it come together.

2. Line a 7x5 baking dish with baking paper and press mixture firmly into dish with a spatula until dough is even. Set in the freezer for 10 minutes. Cut into 12 bite size pieces. Optional to spread on protein frosting. Store in fridge for 5-7 days.

Protein Frosting

Use this recipe on any brownie or cake recipe in this book for a secretly protein-packed frosting!

INGREDIENTS

1/4 cup protein powder of choice *(Natural Road)*
1/4 cup unsweetened vanilla almond milk
1 tsp coconut oil, melted *(Organic Road)*
1/4 tsp cinnamon *(Organic Road)*

METHOD

1. Stir together all ingredients until well combined. Use a spatula to spread onto brownies or cake.

Gooey Crunch
Granola Bars

VEGAN | MAKES 16

These are seriously the quickest and easiest granola bars to whip up in no time! You can be super flexible and creative with your own ingredients and try out different fruit and nut combos.

INGREDIENTS

1 cup (130g) hemp seeds
(13 Seeds)

1 cup (170g) activated buckinis

1 1/2 cup (200g) dried fruit
(I use an antioxidant rich mix of goji berries, blueberries and raspberries)

1/2 cup (45g) shredded coconut
(Organic Road)

1 tsp vanilla

1 tsp cinnamon *(Organic Road)*

1 cup (340g) liquid sweetener
(maple, honey, rice malt syrup)
(Organic Road)

METHOD

1. Preheat oven to 180ºC/350ºF

2. Mix all dry ingredients in bowl, then stir through sweetener until combined and sticky.

3. Spread and press mixture evenly down onto lined baking tray using a spatula. Place in oven to 12-15 minutes until golden brown (it can burn quickly, so keep an eye on it!)

NUTRITIONAL INFO

210 CALORIES / 7G PROTEIN / 54G CARBS / 10G FAT / 1G DIETARY FIBRE PER SERVE

Quick & easy snack

Zesty Berry Bread

LOW CARB | MAKES 12

Lemon and berries is my favourite combo in any dessert,
and is no exception in this fluffy, filling dessert bread!

INGREDIENTS

1 1/2 cups almond flour

4 eggs, separated

1/2 cup coconut sugar or
xylitol for sugar-free
(Organic Road)

2 tbsp lemon zest, finely grated

1 cup frozen or fresh blueberries

Optional topping: 1/4 cup flaked
almonds

Optional for serving: icing sugar
and lemon slices for garnish

NUTRITIONAL INFO

61 CALORIES / 3G PROTEIN /
7G CARBS / 3G FAT / 1G DIETARY
FIBRE PER SERVE

METHOD

1. Preheat your oven to 180°C/360°F. Grease and line a loaf pan.

2. In a mixing bowl, combine 4 egg yolks and your sweetener of choice and beat by hand or with an electric beater until thick and creamy and lightened in colour.

3. Add almond flour and lemon zest and use a spatula to fold mixture until well combined.

4. In another mixing bowl, use an electric beater add 4 egg whites and beat together until stiff peaks form (you will need an electric beater). Fold the egg whites one spoonful at a time into the almond meal mixture until you have an even consistency.

5. Once all the egg whites are in and the mixture is smooth, transfer into a prepared loaf tin and sprinkle with almonds. Bake 30 mins or until a skewer inserted comes out clean.

Spiced Dessert Bread

PALEO | MAKES 12 SLICES

A wholesome, fluffy and macro-friendly dessert bread packed with antioxidant-rich spices and hidden veggies: zucchini, which you won't be able to taste at all!

INGREDIENTS

1 cup grated zucchini

1 1/2 cup almond flour

1/4 cup maple syrup
(Organic Road)

3 whole eggs

1 tbsp coconut oil
(Organic Road)

1 1/2 tsp cinnamon
(Organic Road)

1 1/2 tsp vanilla extract

1 tsp baking powder

1/4 tsp salt *(Natural Road)*

Optional: 1/2 cup cocoa powder and 1/2 cup chocolate chips to hide the zucchini!

METHOD

1. Preheat the oven to 180°C/360°F. Line a bread pan with baking paper.

2. Combine all of the ingredients for the bread (except the zucchini) in a mixing bowl or KitchenAid mixer.

3. Grate the zucchini and add it into the batter.

4. Once the batter is combined and smooth, pour it into the loaf pan.

5. Bake the loaf for about 1 hour and 5 minutes, or until golden brown on top and a skewer inserted comes out clean.

NUTRITIONAL INFO

69 CALORIES / 2G PROTEIN / 6G CARBS / 4G FAT / 1G DIETARY FIBRE PER SERVE

Hidden Veggies!

Hemp Protein Banana Bread

I'm bready for the day

VEGAN | FLOURLESS | REFINED SUGAR-FREE | MAKES 14 SLICES

Everyone needs a staple healthy banana bread in their recipe arsenal, and this one is the one you'll make over and over again. Packed with complete protein from nutritious hemp seeds, this is a great breakfast on the go or healthy power snack!

INGREDIENTS

2 1/2 cups (250g) rolled oats *(Organic Road)*

1 3/4 cups (420g) banana, mashed *(about 3-4 bananas)*

1/3 cup (80g) milk of choice OR olive oil *(Cobram Estate)*

1/2 cup (170g) liquid sweetener *(maple syrup, agave, or honey) (Organic Road)*

Optional: 1 1/2 tbsp apple cider vinegar*

1/4 cup (30g) hemp seeds *(13 Seeds)*

1/2 tsp cinnamon *(Organic Road)*

1 tsp baking soda

3/4 tsp baking powder

1/2 tsp salt *(Natural Road)*

1 1/2 tsp vanilla extract

NUTRITIONAL INFO

102 CALORIES / 4G PROTEIN / 21.7G CARBS / 1.1G FAT / 2G DIETARY FIBRE PER SERVE

METHOD

1. Preheat oven to 175°C/350°F fan-forced, line and grease a 9×5 loaf pan very well, making sure to go up the sides.

2. Place the oats in a blender or food processor and blitz until it is a fine flour consistency. Add all other ingredients escept hemp seeds, and blend until smooth. Pour the batter into the prepared pan, then sprinkle on the hemp seeds. Bake on the middle rack for 35 minutes. Turn the oven off, but DON'T open the oven. Let the bread sit in the closed oven for another 10 minutes. Then remove from the oven and let cool completely before slicing.

NOTES

- Vinegar reacts with the baking soda and helps it rise, but the recipe still works great without. Any vinegar can be used. You can also use lemon juice OR add two teaspoons of additional baking powder.

- It is topped with Hemp "Butter" on page 234.

- Optional to stir in 1/2 cup mini chocolate chips, and extra hemp seeds.

1 Bowl Vegan Brownies

MAKES 12 BROWNIES

These are my favourite ever baked vegan brownies!
Full of healthy fats and antioxidants, you can't go
wrong with this healthy pleantbased treat.

INGREDIENTS

**2 cups (300g) dates, pitted,
soaked in hot water for 10
minutes** *(measured after pitting)*

**1/4 cup date water, reserved
from soaking the dates**

1/2 cup (125g) peanut butter*
*(if unsalted, add a pinch of
salt to the batter)*

**2 tbsp (20g) olive or
coconut oil, melted***
(Cobram Estate)

**1/3 cup (40g) cacao
or cocoa powder** *(Organic Road)*

**Optional: 1/3 cup sugar-free
dark chocolate chips**
(I use Well Naturally)

**Optional: 1/2 cup roughly
chopped raw walnuts**

NUTRITIONAL INFO

163 CALORIES / 3G PROTEIN
/ 23G CARBS / 8G FAT / 3G
DIETARY FIBRE PER SERVE

METHOD

1. Preheat oven to 175°C/350°F and line a loaf
   pan with baking paper. Set aside.

2. Add dates to food processor and blend until
   small bits or a ball forms. Add hot water and
   blend until a sticky date paste forms. Scrape
   down sides as needed.

3. Add peanut butter, coconut oil, and cacao
   powder and pulse until a sticky batter forms. It
   should be tacky and thick (scrape down sides
   as needed). Lastly add chocolate chips and
   walnuts (optional) and pulse to incorporate.

4. Transfer batter to lined loaf pan and spread
   into an even layer. For a smooth top, lay some
   parchment paper on top and use a flat-
   bottomed object (like a drinking glass)
   to press into an even layer.

5. Bake on the center rack for 15 minutes – the
   edges should be slightly dry. Remove from
   oven and let cool in the pan for 10 minutes.
   Then carefully lift out of the pan using the
   edges of the parchment paper and let cool on
   a plate or cooling rack for at least 20 minutes
   before slicing. They will firm up as they cool.
   Store leftovers covered at room temperature
   up to 3 days, in the refrigerator up to 5-6 days,
   or in the freezer up to 1 month (let thaw before
   enjoying). Enjoy warm or cool.

My Fave
vegan brownies

Cakes &
Cupcakes

the cover girl

Coco Vanilla & Jam Sponge Cake

PALEO | SUGAR-FREE OPTION | MAKES A 15CM/6 INCH CAKE & 14-16 SLICES

The perfect cake for a tea party - people won't believe it's full of wholefoods! I tripled this recipe to get the shot on the cover of this book and to make it a centrepiece of any dining table. I love all the recipes in this book (of course!) but this one I'm particularly partial to because it took a while to perfect - but the fluffy spongey result was well worth it!

INGREDIENTS

3/4 cup (150g) coconut oil, melted (you can also use butter) *(Organic Road)*

1 cup (150g) coconut sugar or xylitol for sugar-free/non-paleo option *(Organic Road)*

8 eggs

1 tbsp vanilla extract

1 cup (120g) coconut flour *(Organic Road)*

1/2 tsp baking soda

1/2 tsp salt *(Natural Road)*

OPTIONAL TO SERVE

1 cup Coconut "Buttercream" on page 233 or Coconut Whipped Cream on page 233

1 1/2 cup berry chia jam on page 228

NUTRITIONAL INFO

FOR 16 SLICES - 272 CALORIES / 6G PROTEIN / 21G CARBS / 18G FAT / 7G DIETARY FIBRE PER SERVE

METHOD

1. CAKE: Preheat the oven to 175°C/350°F. Line two 6-inch cake pans with baking paper rounds then grease the sides of the pans with oil.

2. In a large bowl, combine the coconut oil, coconut sugar, eggs, and vanilla. Sift in the the coconut flour, baking soda and salt, stir to combine, do not over-mix.

3. Divide the batter evenly among the prepared pans and bake for about 25 minutes, until a skewer inserted into the center comes out clean. Let cool for 10 minutes before removing from pan onto a cooling rack.

4. ASSEMBLY: Place one layer on a plate and top with 1 tablespoon of jam, then 2 tablespoons of coconut buttercream, smoothing each evenly over the entire surface. Add another cake layer, and repeat. Continue until all layers have been used and top the final layer with the remaining jam and coconut whipped cream. Refrigerate until ready to serve.

NOTES

I tripled this recipe for photoshoot purposes, layering the cream, jam and fruit on top of the cake and repeat.

Almond & Pear Tea Cake

GLUTEN-FREE | MAKES 10 SERVINGS

INGREDIENTS

3 eggs

3/4 cup (255g) maple syrup
(Organic Road)

1 tsp vanilla extract

Optional: 1 tsp almond extract

2 cups (200g) almond flour
*(sometimes also called
"almond meal/flour")*

3/4 tsp salt *(Natural Road)*

**1 1/4 cups (about 190g) fresh
pear, peeled and chopped
into bite-size pieces**

NUTRITIONAL INFO

199 CALORIES / 7G PROTEIN
/ 24G CARBS / 9G FAT / 3G
DIETARY FIBRE PER SERVE

METHOD

1. Preheat oven to 175°C/350°F fan-forced. Line and lightly grease an 8-inch spring-form pan.

2. In a large bowl, whisk together eggs, maple syrup, and extracts. Sift in almond meal and salt, stir to combine. Fold in chopped pears.

3. Pour the batter into your prepared pan, and bake for 35-40 minutes, or until caramelized and golden brown on top and a skewer comes out clean when the cake is pierced.

TIPS

- Pineapple or raspberries in place of pear is also amazing in this cake.

- Other add-ins include 1 tbsp of poppyseeds, 1 tablespoon of lemon zest,

- To add some crunch and texture to this tea cake, you can also grind up almonds in place of almond flour.

- I topped the cake with caramelized pear - just boil the pear until soft in the sprinkle with coconut sugar and bake in the oven on a low heat until caramelized.

Flourless Fudgy Chocolate Cake

GLUTEN-FREE | VEGAN | MAKES 10

This vegan flourless cake reminds me of a cross between a rich chocolate truffle and chocolate fudge, with a hint of blueberry sweetness

INGREDIENTS

1 1/4 cup (190g) frozen blueberries, defrosted

1 tsp vanilla extract

3/4 cup (85g) cacao powder
(Organic Road)

1/2 cup (75g) coconut sugar or xylitol for sugar-free
(Organic Road)

1 tbsp baking powder

NUTRITIONAL INFO

70 CALORIES / 2G PROTEIN / 17G CARBS / 1G FAT / 3G DIETARY FIBRE PER SERVE

METHOD

1. Preheat oven to 175°C/350°F fan-forced. Line and lightly grease an 8-inch spring-form pan.

2. Add blueberries to a pan and bring to a boil, stirring and mashing for 2 minutes. Lower to medium heat and cook for another 4 minutes until thickened. Place blueberries and vanilla in food processor blender and blend until pureed.

3. Whisk together the cacao powder, sweetener, and baking powder in a bowl, then pour into the food processor and process until combined and smooth.

4. Spread evenly into a 6 inch pan lined with parchment paper. Bake for 25 minutes Let the cake cool for at least 20 minutes before removing from the pan. It is very delicate when warm, so to be sure it comes out cleanly, you can chill the cake first. Serve warm or cold, it's delicious both ways!

Blueberry Skillet Friand Cake

VEGAN OPTIONS | MAKES 12 SERVES

Perfect for making the most out of berry season, this 5 ingredient blueberry skillet cake is the easy dessert recipe you've been waiting to enjoy! Best of all, there's no washing, and it looks lovely and unique presented in the skillet.

INGREDIENTS

1 cup (150g) flour
(all purpose or whole wheat pastry flour or gluten-free flour)
(Organic Road)

1 cup (120g) coconut sugar or xylitol for sugar-free
(Organic Road)

1 cup (240g) milk of choice

1/2 cup (125g) butter or vegan butter

2 cup frozen or fresh blueberries

NUTRITIONAL INFO

181 CALORIES / 2.2G PROTEIN / 24G CARBS / 9.1G FAT / 0.9 DIETARY FIBRE PER SERVE

METHOD

1. Preheat oven to 160°C/375°F, lightly grease a skillet with cooking spray, oil or butter and set aside.

2. In a large bowl melt the butter then whisk in the flour, sugar and milk to combine, until] smooth. Pour into the prepared skillet. Sprinkle the blueberries evenly around the top of the batter.

3. Bake for 40-45 minutes, or until edges start to turn slightly brown. Remove from oven and allow to cool for 10 minutes

NOTES

I used a 10 1/4 inch skillet for this recipe. You could use a smaller skillet, the cake would just be a little taller!

Molten Lava Chocolate Cake

KETO | LOW CARB | SUGAR-FREE | GLUTEN-FREE | MAKES 2

A deliciously rich low carb chocolate lava cake with a gooey molten centre.

INGREDIENTS

1/3 cup (55g) sugar-free dark chocolate, melted *(Well Naturally)*

1/4 cup (55g) coconut oil *(Organic Road)*

2 eggs, beaten

2 tbsp desiccated coconut or almond flour *(Organic Road)*

2 tbsp xylitol or sweetener of choice *(Organic Road)*

NUTRITIONAL INFO

497 CALORIES / 8G PROTEIN / 9G CARBS / 47G FAT / 8G DIETARY FIBRE PER CAKE

METHOD

1. Preheat oven to 175°C/350°F. Grease 2 ramekins with oil.

2. Stir the chocolate and oil together in a bowl. Stir in the eggs, coconut and sweetener - it will be a dough-like consistency that is pourable.

3. Pour into 2 greased ramekins. Bake 9 minutes until the top is set but still jiggly. Do NOT over-bake!

4. Either turnout onto plates and serve with a dusting of powdered xylitol (just blend the sweetener until it is in a powdered form) and some fresh fruit, such as sliced strawberries or raspberries.

NOTES

- If you want to turn your cakes out, grease your ramekins REALLY WELL! If you are only after the taste, then just serve in the ramekins.

- Do NOT over-bake! The top needs to be set, but jiggly. Don't deprive yourself of that gooey centre.

- Best eaten straight out of the oven! If you leave them in the ramekins for long, they will continue to cook and set more than you might like.

Impressive dessert, minimum fuss.

Apple & Raspberry Galette

SUGAR-FREE | MAKES 10 SERVINGS

A wholesome version of the famous french freeform cake. The rustic aesthetic means it's ok if it's perfectly imperfect! Designed to be shared, and guaranteed to be completely devoured with no leftovers.

INGREDIENTS

Pastry

2 cups (300g) wholemeal flour *(Organic Road)*

1 tbsp xylitol *(Organic Road)*

100g salted butter, chilled and cubed *(if not salted, add a pinch of salt)*

2 eggs, chilled

1-2 tsp chilled water

Optional: 1 tbsp milk for brushing

Filling

1 cup (about 150g) apple, cored and diced, optional to skin

1 cup (about 150g) strawberries, sliced

Optional: 1/2 cup (60g) xylitol *(I find it sweet enough without)* *(Organic Road)*

NUTRITIONAL INFO

190 CALORIES / 5G PROTEIN / 21.7G CARBS / 9.7G FAT / 3.3G DIETARY FIBRE PER SERVE

METHOD

1. **PASTRY:** Process the flour and Natvia until combined. Add the butter and pulse until it resembles breadcrumbs. Add the eggs and iced water. Pulse about 3x until it just starts to come together. Roll into a ball before flattening into a disk. Cover in plastic wrap and chill for 30 minutes.

2. **FILLING:** Boil the apple in a saucepan with 1/4 cup water. Lower to simmer, and add the strawberries. Cook for about 5 mins until the apple is softened. Stir through Natvia if using.

3. **ASSEMBLY:** Roll out the dough between 2 sheets of baking paper, into an oval shape, about 3mm thick. Spread the fruit mixture in the middle, and fold up the edges of the pastry. Optional to brush edges with a whisked egg white for shine, and sprinkle with sweetener.

4. **BAKE:** for 18-20 minutes at 180°C/360°F in a fan-forced oven for 18-20 minutes or until golden brown.

TIPS

Before rolling out the dough, reserve 1/4 of the pastry to use to make shapes for decoration. Stars are festive for Christmas or hearts for a special occasion.

Perfectly Imperfect

Failproof

Vegan Cheesecake

VEGAN | GLUTEN-FREE | MAKES 12 SLICES

This will be your new go-to, fail-proof cheesecake recipe - the flavours and textures are so incredibly rich and creamy, without the unnecessary fats, sugars and oils in conventional cheesecake. I recommend making a day in advance before serving, as the flavours and textures intensify.

INGREDIENTS

OPTIONAL CRUST

1 1/2 cup (150g) almond flour *(or pulse nuts to make flour)*

4 tbsp (40g) coconut oil, melted or water if avoiding oil *(Organic Road)*

1/4 tsp salt *(Natural Road)*

CHEESECAKE

2 packets (500g) cream cheese or vegan cream cheese, room temp

2 cups (500g) yogurt or coconut milk yogurt

2 1/2 tsp vanilla extract

Optional: 1 tbsp lemon juice

2/3 cup xylitol *(sugar or maple syrup also work for non-keto)* *(Organic Road)*

1/4 cup almond flour

OPTIONAL TOPPING

Fresh berries

METHOD

1. **CRUST:** combine all crust ingredients in a food processor until sticky and press down onto an 6-inch springform cake pan.

2. **CHEESECAKE:** Preheat oven to 175°C/350°F fan-forced. Fill any baking pan about halfway up with water, and place it on the oven's lower rack. Beat all cheesecake ingredients in a blender or food processor just until smooth (overbeating can cause cracking as it bakes). Pour filling on top of prepared crust or bought crust. Place on the middle rack (above the rack with the water pan). Bake 25 minutes and do not open the oven at all during this time. Once time is up, still do not open the oven, but turn off the heat and let the cheesecake sit in the oven an additional 5 minutes. Then remove from the oven - it will still look underdone. Let cool on the counter 20 minutes, then refrigerate overnight, during which time it will firm up. It is important the cake cools gradually and thus does not crack. Store leftovers covered in the refrigerator 3–4 days, or slice and freeze if desired.

NUTRITIONAL INFO

185 CALORIES / 7G PROTEIN / 9G CARBS / 15G FAT / 0G DIETARY FIBRE PER SLICE

Banana Blender Muffins
- 15 ways

GLUTEN-FREE | FLOURLESS | VEGAN | MAKES 6 MUFFINS

These are the easiest, most delicious muffins you'll ever make. They boast a clean-eating ingredient list and are made without any flour, oil, or refined sugar. Use the base recipe and then check out the many variations you can create. The base recipe makes 12 mini-muffins, but can easily be doubled to prep nourishing snacks for a busy week.

INGREDIENTS

1/2 cup peanut butter or nut/seed butter of choice *(Organic Road)*

1 medium ripe banana

1 large egg or flax egg*
(Organic Road ground flaxseed)

1/2 tsp vanilla extract

2 tbso honey or maple syrup
(Organic Road)

1/2 tsp baking powder

NUTRITIONAL INFO

182 CALORIES / 7.9G PROTEIN / 13.3G CARBS / 11.6G FAT / 31.9G DIETARY FIBRE PER MUFFIN

METHOD

1. Preheat the oven to 180°C/360°F

2. Spray your muffin tin with cooking oil and set aside.

3. Place all ingredients in a blender and blend until very smooth.

4. Fill each muffin cup until just a little more than halfway

5. Bake in the pre-heated oven for 15 to 20 minutes or until muffins are golden brown on the outside and cooked on the inside (check this by using a skewer stick to poke through to check).

6. Let the muffins cool completely before removing from the muffin pan and enjoy!

TIPS

* Combine 1 tablespoon flaxseed meal with 3 tablespoons water in a small bowl and let it sit for a few minutes to form a gel. Substitute this "flax egg" for the real egg in the base recipe.

- **Sunbutter (nut-free):** Substitute sunflower seed butter for the peanut butter.

- **Sunbutter Crunch (nut-free):** Substitute sunflower seed butter for the peanut butter and top each mini-muffin with a sprinkle of sunflower seeds.

- **Almond Butter:** Substitute almond butter for the peanut butter.

- **Almond Butter White Chocolate Chip:** Substitute almond butter for the peanut butter and stir 1/4-1/2 cup white chocolate chips into the batter, or top the muffins with the chips after your pour the batter into the muffin tin.

- **Lime:** add 2 tablespoons of lime juice to the batter. Top each muffin with lime zest.

- **Peanut Butter and Jelly:** Fill the muffin tin one-third of the way with batter. Put about 1/4 teaspoon of raspberry chia seed jam on page 228 or your favorite jam/jelly in the center, then fill the muffin cup to almost the top with more batter.

- **Blueberry:** Add 1/2 cup wild blueberries to the batter, or top each muffin cup with blueberries.

- **Mango:** Add 1/2 cup diced mango to the batter, or top each muffin cup with the diced mango.

- **Pineapple:** Add 1/2 cup diced pineapple to the batter or top each muffin cup with the diced pineapple.

- **Cinnamon:** Follow the base recipe, but sprinkle the tops of the muffins with cinnamon. I like plain cinnamon, but you could do a mixture of cinnamon and coconut sugar. I use a fine mesh strainer to get an even, fine sprinkle of cinnamon.

- **Coconut:** Sprinkle the top of the muffins with unsweetened shredded coconut.

- **Chocolate Chip:** Add 1/4-1/2 cup chocolate chips or mini chips to the batter or on top of the muffins.

- **Raisin:** Add 1/2 cup raisins to the batter or to the top of the muffins.

- **Lemon & Poppyseed:** Add 2 tbsp lemon zest finely grated and use cashew butter instead of peanut butter.

Choc Mousse Tart

VEGAN | PROTEIN | SERVES 14

A protein-packed chocolate tart with a secret superfood ingredient: tofu! Don't worry, you won't be able to taste it, the ingredients will transform into a rich, velvety mousse that tastes naughty (but is not!) You can also buy your own base if you don't want to make your own, however this base is only 3 ingredients and ridiculously easy!

INGREDIENTS

OPTIONAL BASE OR YOU BUY YOUR OWN

2 cups (250g) walnuts

1 heaping cup (~16) dates*, pitted

1/4 cup raw cacao powder
(Organic Road)

MOUSSE

1 block (90g) sugar-free dark chocolate**, melted
(Well Naturally)

1 can coconut cream *(frozen for 1 hour)* *(Organic Road)*

1 packet (400g) silken tofu
(Organic Road)

1/2 cup maple syrup
(Organic Road)

1 tsp vanilla essence

OPTIONAL TOPPING

Pomegranate seeds

METHOD

1. **BASE:** To make the base, pulse the walnuts and cacao into flour in a food processor. Add the dates and process until they stick together. Press down into tart pan or cake pan.

2. **MOUSSE:** Blend all mousse ingredients, pour into base and freeze for 1-2 hours, or refrigerate overnight.

NOTES

*Soak dates in boiling water for 10 minutes if dry. If you don't want to use dates, use the base recipe that the Vegan Cheesecake uses on page 133

**Use dairy-free chocolate if vegan.

NUTRITIONAL INFO

163 CALORIES / 3G PROTEIN / 21G CARBS / 6G FAT / 2G DIETARY FIBRE PER TART

Chocolate Bundt Cake

VEGAN | MAKES 12-15 SERVES

A Bundt cake is a cake that is baked in a Bundt pan, that is a distinctive doughnut shape. This is a delicious basic chocolate cake that is super versatile for whatever toppings you wish!

INGREDIENTS

1 cup (150g) self-raising flour
(if not self-raising, add 1 ½ tsp baking powder)

1/2 cup (75g) coconut sugar
or xylitol for sugar-free
(Organic Road)

1/2 cup (45g) desiccated coconut
(Organic Road)

1/2 cup (60g) cacao or cocoa
powder *(Organic Road)*

1 cup (240g) milk of choice

METHOD

1. Preheat oven to 180°C/360°F.

2. Place all ingredients in a bowl and mix. Line a loaf tin with baking paper and pour mixture in. Bake for 40 minutes.

NOTES

I topped my Bundt cake with caramel sauce on page 236 and salted caramel coconut chips on page 198

NUTRITIONAL INFO

77 CALORIES / 2.7G PROTEIN
/ 18.2G CARBS / 3.1G FAT / 5.3
DIETARY FIBRE PER SERVE

Bundt pans create beautiful cakes effortlessly!

Chickpea Chocolate Cake

GLUTEN-FREE | SERVES 10

The BEST sugar-free flourless chocolate cake recipe you'll ever try, that's secretly full of nutritious, fibre-packed chickpeas. No one will ever know this decadent chocolate cake is full of heart-healthy legumes!

INGREDIENTS

1½ cups Sugar-Free Dark Chocolate (250g) *(Well Naturally)*

1½ can chickpeas or Cannelini Beans, drained and rinsed

4 Whole Eggs or 3 Whole Eggs & 2 Egg Whites *(egg whites weighing 50g)*

1/2 cup coconut sugar or xylitol (65g) *(Organic Road)*

1/3 cup cacao or cocoa powder (20g) *(Organic Road)*

½ tsp baking soda

1/2 tsp cinnamon *(Organic Road)*

1/4 tsp salt *(Natural Road)*

3/4 tsp vanilla extract

METHOD

1. Preheat the oven to 180ºC/350ºF fan-forced.

2. Melt the chocolate in the microwave or in a heat-proof bowl over a saucepan of boiling water.

3. Process the chickpeas and eggs in a food processor until very smooth. Add the sweetener and baking soda and pulse until combined. Add the melted chocolate and blend until smooth.

4. Pour the mixture into a greased and lined baking tin and bake for 25 minutes. Allow to cool for 15 minutes, then remove from tin and drizzle chocolate or dust icing sugar on the top.

NUTRITIONAL INFO

202 CALORIES / 7G PROTEIN / 10G CARBS / 14G FAT / 9G DIETARY FIBRE PER SERVE

Lemon Blueberry Muffins

HIGH PROTEIN | MAKES 12

*Fresh lemon and juicy blueberries make these healthy,
lemon blueberry muffins a sweet, yet wholesome
5-ingredient treat. Top them with creamy Greek yogurt
or coconut cream "buttercream" on page 233 for the
perfect protein-packed pre-or-post-workout snack!*

INGREDIENTS

6 eggs OR 340g liquid egg whites

2 1/2 cup (250g) rolled oats
(Organic Road)

1/2 cup (90g) non-fat Greek
yoghurt

1 lemon, juice + zest

1/2 cup blueberries *{add to
mixture after blended}*

Optional: 2 tbsp sweetener of
choice - I personally prefer no
sweetener as the berries are
sweet enough!

NUTRITIONAL INFO

EGG WHITES: 102 CALORIES / 6G
PROTEIN / 15G CARBS / 2G FAT /
1G DIETARY FIBRE PER SERVE

WHOLE EGGS: 124 CALORIES / 6G
PROTEIN / 15G CARBS / 4G FAT /
1G DIETARY FIBRE PER SERVE

METHOD

1. Preheat oven to 175 C/350F, grease muffin
   tin if needed {I suggest using a silicon muffin
   pan} and set aside.

2. In a high-speed blender, combine whole
   eggs or liquid egg whites, oats, Greek yogurt,
   lemon juice, and lemon zest to taste.

3. Blend until mixture is smooth.

4. Stir in blueberries {you can always substitute
   frozen blueberries too}.

5. Divide mixture evenly into 12 muffin cups.

6. Top with additional blueberries and rolled
   oats if desired.

7. Bake for 20-25 minutes until tops are lightly
   golden brown or toothpick can be inserted in
   muffin and come out clean.

8. Let muffins cool and top with additional
   Greek Yogurt, blueberries, and lemon zest if
   desired.

9. Store leftover muffins in air-tight glass
   container in the fridge or freezer.

Apple Crumble

VEGAN | MAKES 2 SERVES

This isn't a traditional Apple Crumble. It's a ridiculously easy recipe I've made over and over for last minute treats and dinner parties; it's as quick to make as it is to consume. This will be your go-to weeknight dessert, combining a serve of fruit (or so we tell ourselves) with a simple crumble topping.

INGREDIENTS

Filling:

1 apple, peeled, cored, and sliced into small cubes

1 tbsp (10g) coconut sugar
(Organic Road)

1/4 tsp cinnamon *(Organic Road)*

Topping:

1/3 cup + 2 tbsp (40g) rolled oats
(Organic Road)

2 tbsp (25g) coconut sugar
(Organic Road)

2 tbsp (30g) vegan butter, melted
(butter if not vegan)

METHOD

1. Preheat oven to 180°C/350°F.

2. Filling: In a bowl, toss apples with sugar and cinnamon. Divide apples into 2 individual ramekins, and press them slightly. Set aside.

3. Topping: Process 2 tbsp of the rolled oats until it is a flour consistency (oat flour). Mix oats, oat flour and sugar, then mix in melted butter until mixture clumps together into crumbly balls. Sprinkle crumble evenly on top of the apple mixture.

4. Bake for about 30 minutes, until topping is golden brown and apples are tender. Serve warm and top with icecream and crushed nuts if desired!

NUTRITIONAL INFO

308 CALORIES / 3.1G PROTEIN / 46.7G CARBS / 13.7G FAT / 4.9G DIETARY FIBRE PER SERVE

No-Bake Chocolate Lasagna

KETO | MAKES 16

You'll love this chocolate version of lasagna! Each layer has less than 5 ingredients and can be consumed by itself, but I loved the idea of combining multiple Nourish in 5 recipes in one and creating a dessert lasagna!

INGREDIENTS

Brownie Layer:

1 cup (300g) nut or seed butter of choice *(Organic Road)*

2/3 cup (80g) cocoa powder *(Organic Road)*

4-5 tbsp xylitol, or to taste *(Organic Road)*

1/4 cup (45g) sugar-free dark chocolate, melted *(Well Naturally)*

1/4 tsp salt *(Natural Road)*

1 tsp vanilla

Cream Layer:

2 packet silken tofu (900g)

3/4 cup (90g) powdered sweetener of choice* - I use Xylitol to keep it sugar-free *(Organic Road)*

1/4 cup (40g) coconut oil or vegan butter, melted *(Organic Road)*

2 tsp vanilla extract

Choc Mousse Layer:

1 can full fat coconut cream, only scoop out the cream *(Organic Road)*

2-4 tbsp powdered sweetener of choice, to taste - I use Xylitol to keep it sugar-free *(Organic Road)*

3 tbsp cocoa powder *(Organic Road)*

1/4 tsp salt *(Natural Road)*

2/3 cup coconut cream** *(Organic Road)*

METHOD

1. BROWNIE LAYER Blend everything together in a food processor - scraping down the sides as needed - until it forms a smooth dough. Press into baking dish. Place in the freezer whilst you make the other layers.

2. CREAM LAYER: Put all cream layer ingredients in a food processor and blend until the mixture is creamy. Pour HALF of the cream onto the brownie layer, and place the whole baking dish into the freezer for about 20 minutes.

3. CHOC MOUSSE LAYER: Heat up coconut cream and sweetener of choice in a pan until it begins to simmer. Turn off the heat and thoroughly stir in the cocoa and salt. Allow to cool completely (you can do a water bath to speed up the process). Smooth on top of the baking dish.

4. Finally, top off the choc mousse layer with the other half the cream layer. Top with choc chips or chocolate shavings if desired. Store leftovers in the fridge for up to 4 days.

TIPS

- You can use dairy-free or soy-free cream cheese instead of silken tofu, however, most brands contain a lot of fat. So, if you use store-bought cream cheese, you can omit the coconut oil. Depending on the thickness of the cream cheese you might need to add a splash of plant-based milk to thin out the cream cheese.

- *To powder your sweetener, simply put sweetener in your high-speed food processor and mix for a few seconds until it's a fine powder.

NUTRITIONAL INFO

BROWNIE LAYER WITH CASHEW NUT BUTTER - 156 CALORIES / 4G PROTEIN / 12G CARBS / 10G FAT / 2G DIETARY FIBRE PER SERVE

CREAM LAYER - 70 CALORIES / 2G PROTEIN / 1G CARBS / 4G FAT / 0G DIETARY FIBRE PER SERVE

CHOCOLATE MOUSSE - 76 CALORIES / 0G PROTEIN / 9G CARBS / 5G FAT / 0G DIETARY FIBRE PER SERVE

each layer is delicious by itself

Peanut Butter & Jelly Keto Cheesecake

KETO | VEGAN OPTIONS | GLUTEN-FREE | MAKES 16 SERVES

Creamy keto cheesecake in one of my favourite flavour pairings (peanut butter and jelly!) You can of course omit the crust and just have the cheesecake by itself.

INGREDIENTS

Crust

1 1/2 cups (150g) almond flour

1/3 cup (40g) cacao powder
(Organic Road)

1/4 cup (30g) xylitol
(Organic Road)

1/4 cup coconut oil or butter, melted

Cheesecake filling

680g/24 oz cream cheese, room temp

1 1/4 cup (300g) cream cheese OR yogurt of choice for lighter option (coconut, almond milk, greek yoghurt all work)

3/4 cup peanut butter (195g)

2 1/2 tsp vanilla extract

2/3 cup (80g) xylitol

Topping:

1/2 cup berry chia jam (page 228) and optional 1/2 cup peanut butter

NUTRITIONAL INFO

WITH CREAM CHEESE - 193 CALORIES / 13G PROTEIN / 16G CARBS / 10G FAT / 2G DIETARY FIBRE PER SERVE

METHOD

1. **CRUST:** Combine all crust ingredients in a food processor, pour into a lined 8 or 9-inch springform pan, press down firmly and evenly, set aside while you make the filling.

2. **CHEESECAKE FILLING:** Preheat oven to 175°C/ 350°F. Fill any baking pan halfway up with water, and place it on the oven's lower rack. Combine all ingredients except topping in a food processor until just smooth (overbeating can cause cracking as it bakes). Pour filling on top of crust. Dollop jam and peanut butter on top and swirl a pattern with a skewer if desired. Place on the middle rack (above the rack with the water pan). Bake 30 minutes and do not open the oven at all during this time. Once time is up, still do not open the oven, and turn off the heat and let the cheesecake sit in the oven an additional 5 minutes. Remove from the oven 0 it will still look underdone. Let cool for 20 minutes, then refrigerate overnight, during which time it will firm up considerably. It is important the cake cools gradually so it does not crack. Store leftovers covered in the refrigerator 3-4 days, or slice and freeze if desired.

NOTES

Use vegan cream cheese for vegan option.

Keto Chocolate Mudcake

KETO | MAKES 16

This rich and decadent chocolate keto cake is shockingly delicious... Every time I serve it, people always ask for the recipe! It's quite possibly the best chocolate cake you'll make, keto or not keto.

INGREDIENTS

Cake

1 1/2 cups (150g) almond flour

1/2 cup (60g) cacao powder
(Organic Road)

2 1/4 tsp baking powder

1/2 tsp salt *(Natural Road)*

1/3 cup (80g) almond milk

3 eggs

1/3 cup (40g) xylitol
(Organic Road)

1 1/2 tsp vanilla extract

Optional Frosting

1/2 cup cacao powder
(Organic Road)

225g cream cheese

1/4 cup butter

4 cups xylitol

1 1/2 tsp vanilla extract

2-4 tbsp milk of choice

METHOD

1. Preheat oven to 175°C/ 350°F. Line an 8-inch pan. Stir all dry ingredients in a bowl, and all wet ingredients in another bowl, then pour into the dry mix and stir evenly until just combined. Pour into the pan. Bake 15 minutes or until a skewer comes out clean. Let cool completely before frosting.

2. Frosting: combine all ingredients until smooth in a food processor. You may need more or less milk depending on desired consistency.

TIPS

- *For a double layer cake, simply double the recipe and bake in two 8-inch pans.

- To decrease calories, go without the frosting or use less.

NUTRITIONAL INFO

84 CALORIES / 4G PROTEIN / 7G CARBS / 5G FAT / 2G DIETARY FIBRE PER SERVE

Apple Strudel Muffins

MAKES 16 MUFFINS

Tender and flavourful bakery-style cinnamon strudel muffins loaded with tart bites of fresh apple and spiced with cinnamon - you can't go wrong with this as a fab coffee cake, quick breakfast or snack on the run.

INGREDIENTS

Muffins

2 cups (300g) flour of choice
(plain, wholemeal, spelt)
(Organic Road)

1 tsp baking powder

1/2 tsp baking soda

1/2 tsp salt *(Natural Road)*

1/2 cup olive oil or butter, softened
(Cobram Estate)

1 cup (150g) coconut sugar
or xylitol for sugar-free
(Organic Road)

2 eggs

1 1/4 tsp vanilla

1 1/2 cups diced apples

Strudel Topping

1/3 cup coconut sugar
(Organic Road)

1 tbsp flour of choice *(plain, wholemeal, spelt)* *(Organic Road)*

1/4 tsp cinnamon *(Organic Road)*

1 tbsp olive oil or butter
(Cobram Estate)

METHOD

1. Grease or line muffin tin. Preheat oven to 190°C/375°F.

2. Mix the flour, baking powder, baking soda, and salt together in a large bowl.

3. In another bowl, mix together the oil/butter, sugar, vanilla and eggs until you have a smooth batter. Fold in the diced apples, then slowly add in the dry ingredient mixture while stirring. Fill lined muffin cups half-way with batter.

4. In a small bowl, make up the strudel topping. Mix together the coconut sugar, flour, and cinnamon. Stir in the oil/ butter until the mixture resembles large crumbs. Sprinkle the topping over the muffins in the muffin pan.

5. Bake for 20 minutes, or until a toothpick inserted in the center of a muffin comes up clean. Let them muffins sit 5 minutes in the tin before removing to cool. Top with non-fat greek yoghurt if desired.

NUTRITIONAL INFO

185 CALORIES / 3G PROTEIN / 30G CARBS / 8G FAT / 1G DIETARY FIBRE PER SERVE

bakery-style

Keto Vegan Chocolate Mudcake

KETO | VEGAN | MAKES 6 SERVINGS

INGREDIENTS

1 1/2 cups (150g) almond flour

1/3 cup (40g) cacao powder
(Organic Road)

3 flax eggs or eggs
(Organic Road ground flaxseed)

1/3 cup (40g) xylitol
(Organic Road)

2 1/4 tsp baking powder

1/2 tsp salt *(Natural Road)*

1/3 cup water

1 1/2 tsp vanilla extract

NUTRITIONAL INFO

78 CALORIES / 2.7G PROTEIN /
10.2G CARBS / 4.3G FAT / 2.3G
DIETARY FIBRE PER SERVE

METHOD

1. Preheat oven to 175°C/350°F. Grease an 8-inch pan. Stir all ingredients together very well, then pour into the pan. Bake 14–15 minutes until a skewer inserted comes out clean. Let cool completely before frosting.

NOTES

- For a double layer cake, simply double the recipe and bake in two 8-inch pans.

- For the caramel frosting I mixed together the Coconut "Buttercream" Frosting on page 233 and Coconut Sugar Caramel on page 236

- It is topped with Vegan Caramel Chocolate (page 165)

Paleo Sticky Date Pudding

PALEO | REFINED SUGAR-FREE | SERVES 12

Everybody loves a good sticky date pudding, and this recipe is a serious treat - so make sure you invite your friends over!

INGREDIENTS

Pudding

1 cup dates, pitted

1 cup boiling water

1/3 cup coconut sugar
(Organic Road)

2 tbsp butter or olive oil
(Cobram Estate)

2 eggs

1 tsp vanilla extract

1 tsp baking powder

1 1/2 cups (150g) almond meal

To serve

Date Caramel on page 236

METHOD

1. Lightly grease a springform cake tin. In a bowl, soak the dates and boiling water for 10 minutes.

2. Meanwhile, cream the coconut sugar and butter or oil in a food processor or an electric mixer until smooth. Add the eggs and vanilla extract, mix until combined.

3. In a separate bowl mix the almond meal, baking powder and date mixture together.

4. Add the sugar and butter batter and mix until combined. Transfer the batter in to the prepared cake tin and place in to the oven for 40-45 minutes until golden brown, and a skewer inserted comes out clean. Allow to cool for 10 minutes before turning out on to a wire rack. To serve, slice and pour the caramel sauce over the top!

NUTRITIONAL INFO

165 CALORIES / 4.7G PROTEIN / 13.9G CARBS / 10.6G FAT / 2G DIETARY FIBRE PER SERVE

It's a date ;)

157

Chocolate Cravings

Chocolate Salted Caramel Almond Clusters

VEGAN | SUGAR-FREE | GLUTEN-FREE | MAKES 20 SERVES

These babies are rich, decadent and addictive - they're also super quick and easy, with only three ingredients! Makes a beautiful homemade festive gift for a loved one, or a healthy little treat.

INGREDIENTS

2 cups (220g) raw almonds

1/2 tsp salt *(Natural Road)*

150g sugar-free salted caramel chocolate *(Well Naturally)*

Optional: stir through 1/4 cup protein of choice through the chocolate

Optional: Pinch of flaked sea salt for topping

NUTRITIONAL INFO

86 CALORIES / 2G PROTEIN / 2G CARBS / 7G FAT / 3G DIETARY FIBRE PER SERVE

METHOD

1. Preheat oven to 175°C/350°F. Spread almonds on a lined baking tray. Bake for 10-12 minutes until fragrant, Note that the high oil content of almonds will cause it to continue to roast after removal from the oven.

2. Place the chocolate in a large heat-proof bowl over a small pot of boiling water. Once chocolate has melted, add in the almonds and stir until completely covered.

3. Scoop a tablespoon of chocolate-covered almonds from the bowl and drop them in clusters back onto the cooled, lined baking tray. Let cool at room temperature or refrigerate until chocolate has set. Sprinkle with flaked sea salt and serve.

Super
addictive

Protein Peanut Butter Cups

HIGH-PROTEIN | VEGAN | MAKES 8

Inspired by Reese's Peanut Butter Cups, these scrumptious treats are sugar-free and rich in antioxidants from dark chocolate – no one will ever guess they're good for you and packed full of protein! The commercial version contains nasties such as refined sugars, dextrose, hydrogenated vegetable oil and preservatives, while these treats have a handful of clean ingredients!

INGREDIENTS

2 tbsp (30g) powdered sweetener *(I process Organic Road Xylitol until powdered)*

1 scoop (30g) vanilla protein powder *(or unflavoured)* *(Natural Road)*

1/2 cup (130g) smooth peanut butter, melted gently *(add 1/4 tsp salt if unsalted)*

1/2 cup (60g) vegan chocolate or sugar-free dark chocolate (60g) or my Vegan Raw Chocolate on page 165

Optional toppings: freeze-dried strawberries, bee pollen

NUTRITIONAL INFO

90 CALORIES / 5G PROTEIN / 6G CARBS / 4G FAT / 1G DIETARY FIBRE PER SERVE

METHOD

1. Stir together sweetener, protein powder and salt in a bowl. Mix in peanut butter until it becomes a crumbly dough. Add extra protein if it's too liquid, or a dash of water if it's too dry. (Different brands of nut butter yield different results, I use Organic Road)

2. Form dough into ball shapes smaller than your moulds (I use cupcake liners so they look like Reese's Peanut Butter Cups).

3. Melt the chocolate gently on a low heat and prepare 10 cupcake liners. Fill your moulds half-way with the chocolate, place the dough on top then fill the rest of the mould with the chocolate. Optional to add toppings. Set in fridge. Can be stored in fridge or freezer, either way, they're delicious!

NOTES

Well Naturally is my favourite sugar-free brand of chocolate

Raw Vegan
Caramel Chocolate

VEGAN | REFINED SUGAR-FREE | MAKES 20-30 SERVES

I love the creamy, satisfying texture of vegan chocolates! There is a little more effort with this vegan chocolate recipe, as it requires a tempering technique but I assure you it's well worth it. You will need a candy thermometer for this recipe to keep it raw.

INGREDIENTS

(90g) coconut sugar
(Organic Road)

(20g) raw cacao powder
(Organic Road)

1/8 tsp vanilla powder *(or seeds from one vanilla bean)*

1/8 tsp salt *(Natural Road)*

Optional: 1/2 tsp lucuma or maca powder *(adds a subtle caramel flavor*)*

(240g) raw cacao butter

(28g) cacao liquor* *(also known as cacao paste)*

(40g) almond or cashew butter
(Organic Road)

NUTRITIONAL INFO

FOR 25 SERVINGS: 115 CALORIES / 1G PROTEIN / 5G CARBS / 11G FAT / 1G DIETARY FIBRE PER SERVE

METHOD

1. Place the coconut sugar, cocoa powder, vanilla powder, salt and lucuma powder if using in a blender. Blend on high speed for 30 seconds, or until the coconut sugar looks like powdered sugar. Scrape down the sides if needed and blend again. This is important to get a smooth chocolate texture.

2. Fill a medium-size saucepan with about 1 cup of water. Place a heat-proof bowl on top of the saucepan, making sure the bowl doesn't touch the water. Add the cacao butter and cacao liquor to the bowl.

3. Heat over low-medium heat and stir regularly until melted. Make sure the water doesn't come to a boil, you just want to melt the cocoa butter, it should reach a temperature of 42°C/107°F but not higher.

4. Once melted, remove the bowl from the saucepan, but keep the saucepan on the heat (we will need it to reheat the chocolate later). Transfer the melted mixture to the blender. Add the nut butter, and blend on high speed for 20-30 seconds.

5. Transfer to a large mixing bowl and keep stirring using a spatula until the chocolate comes to a temperature of 28°C/82°F. This step will take 15-20 minutes.

6. Once it has cooled down to that temperature, place the mixing bowl on top of the saucepan with the warm water. Keep stirring until the chocolate reaches 87°F (31°C), about 5 minutes. As soon as it has reached this temperature, remove from heat and pour into molds. Your chocolate is now tempered.

7. Let cool at least 3 hours at room temperature before removing from the molds. I don't recommend cooling in the refrigerator as it may cause the chocolate to get white streaks. Chocolate will keep at room temperature for several weeks.

Chocolate Protein Nut Brittle

VEGAN | HIGH-PROTEIN | MAKES 16 SERVINGS

INGREDIENTS

2 cups mixed roasted nuts
(Organic Road)

200g sugar-free milk chocolate
(Well Naturally)

1/4 cup protein powder of choice
(you can omit if you wish)
(Organic Road)

1 tsp olive oil *(Cobram Estate)*

2 tbsp nut butter *(make sure it's drippy, I use Organic Road nut/ seed butter)*

NUTRITIONAL INFO

129 CALORIES / 5G PROTEIN / 5G CARBS / 11G FAT / 0G DIETARY FIBRE PER SERVE

METHOD

1. Roughly crush nuts by pulsing briefly in food processor or with a knife on a chopping board.

2. Spread nuts onto a baking tray lined with a reusable mat. Set aside.

3. Melt chocolate gently on low heat in a microwave or double boiler method. Pour chocolate over nuts to completely cover. Drizzle with nut butter.

4. Place in fridge 2 hours or freezer for 20 minutes. Break into pieces and enjoy! Store in an airtight container in the fridge.

NOTES

Get creative with the chocolate topping - why not try drizzling one of your favourite caramel recipes from the Crazy for Caramel list? (page 236)

I'm nuts
about you

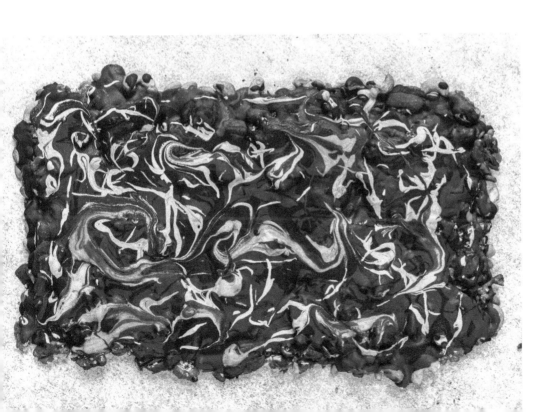

Snickers Protein Fudge

VEGAN | HIGH-PROTEIN | MAKES 12 SERVES

Protein fudge inspired by Snickers, only this version is loaded with healthy fats and protein.

INGREDIENTS

1/4 cup + 1 tbsp (60g) coconut oil
(Organic Road)

1/4 cup (55g) peanut butter

2 tbsp (20g) cacao powder
(Organic Road)

1/4 cup chocolate protein powder (30g)

2 tsp (40g) maple syrup *(optional)*
(Organic Road)

Optional mix ins: roasted peanuts, choc chips

NUTRITIONAL INFO

93 CALORIES / 3G PROTEIN / 5G CARBS / 9G FAT / 1G DIETARY FIBRE PER SERVE

METHOD

1. Combine coconut oil and peanut butter in a microwave-safe bowl and microwave on low setting until coconut oil and peanut butter melt, approximately 15-20 seconds.

2. Stir cocoa powder into coconut oil mixture. Add protein powder and stir to combine. Add maple syrup if additional sweetness is desired.

3. Quickly pour mixture into a mini muffin tin, filling cups about a third of the way to the top. Optional: Mix some peanut flour with water/melt some peanut butter until smooth consistency and drizzle it over the fudge, using a toothpick or knife to swirl it around.

4. Freeze until fudge hardens. Remove from muffin tin and enjoy! Store remaining fudge in the freezer or refrigerator.

Grown-Up Freckles

VEGAN | MAKES 30 FRECKLES

INGREDIENTS

180g sugar-free dark chocolate, chopped *(Well Naturally)*

1/2 cup Superfood Sprinkles on page 238

1 heaped tbsp hemp seeds
(13 Seeds)

NUTRITIONAL INFO

35 CALORIES / 0.5G PROTEIN / 0.4G CARBS / 3.2G FAT / 1.5G DIETARY FIBRE PER SERVE

METHOD

1. Line a baking tray with a reusable baking mat. Place chocolate in microwave-proof bowl and microwave for 1-2 minutes until melted. Stir until smooth.

2. Spoon about 1 tbs chocolate onto tray, shaping into a round. Repeat to make 20 chocolate circles. Scatter with the hemp seeds and Superfood Sprinkles, then chill for 1 hour or until set. Store in an airtight container.

TIPS

*You can also use mixed freeze-dried fruit instead of the Superfood Sprinkles (such as mango, strawberry and apple - from health food aisle at supermarkets)

Frozen 'n' Chilled

Peanut Butter Pudding

VEGAN | LOW CARB | MAKES 14 SMALL SERVES

INGREDIENTS

1 can/3 cups full-fat coconut milk or cream *(Organic Road)*

4 Tbsp arrowroot or corn starch

5-6 tbsp maple syrup *(Organic Road)*

1 cup (250g) peanut butter *(add 1/4 tsp salt if unsalted)*

1 tsp vanilla extract

OPTIONAL FOR SERVING

Coconut whipped cream

Crushed peanuts

Melted sugar-free chocolate

NUTRITIONAL INFO

274 CALORIES / 4G PROTEIN / 16G CARBS / 23G FAT / 1G DIETARY FIBRE PER SERVE

METHOD

1. Whisk coconut milk and starch in a large saucepan, until smooth. Turn pan on over medium heat until bubbly and thickened (approximately 5 minutes).

2. Remove saucepan from heat and stir in maple syrup, peanut butter and vanilla, taste and adjust amounts to your preference.

3. Pour mixture into a medium mixing bowl (glass is best) and let cool on the countertop for 10 minutes. Cover mixing bowl with baking paper so that it touches the surface of the pudding (to prevent a film)

4. Chill overnight in the fridge (or until thickened and cold). Serve with optional toppings. Store leftovers covered in the refrigerator up to 5 days.

Raffaello Coconut
Cookie Dough

PROTEIN | VEGAN | SUGAR-FREE | GLUTEN-FREE | LOW CARB | KETO | MAKES 4 SERVES

If Raffaello were to make a Cookie Dough dessert, it would taste exactly like this! Unlike the original, it's packed with healthy fats and protein to keep you fuller for longer and kick those sugar-cravings!

INGREDIENTS

2 scoop protein powder (60g)
(Organic Road)

2/3 cup (60g) shredded coconut
(Organic Road)

1/4 cup (24g) coconut flour
(Organic Road)

1/4 tsp salt *(Natural Road)*

1/4 tsp vanilla essence

1 tbsp xylitol (20g) *(Organic Road)*

1/2 cup + 1 tbsp water*

1/4 cup dark or white choc chips (50g) *(Well Naturally)*

METHOD

1. Combine all ingredients in a bowl and stir together. Wait a minute or so for the coconut flour to absorb the moisture of the wet ingredients, then stir again. Taste and adjust for sweetener. Mix through choc chips if desired.

NOTES

*You can use Organic Road canned coconut milk for extra creaminess if not concerned about calories.

NUTRITIONAL INFO

271 CALORIES / 14G PROTEIN / 14G CARBS / 14G FAT / 4G DIETARY FIBRE PER SERVE

Caramilk Fudge

VEGAN | REFINED SUGAR-FREE | RAW | MAKES 20 SMALL SERVES

A healthified raw version of the viral Aussie chocolate, Caramilk. You can use any mold you wish, I've used a spoon mold because I LOVE having this melted in coffee.

INGREDIENTS

1 cup (192g) coconut sugar + 1/4 cup (60ml) water *(Organic Road)*

1 cup (225g) raw cacao butter

1 cup raw cashews or macadamias

1 tsp vanilla extract

1/2 tsp salt *(Natural Road)*

NUTRITIONAL INFO

174 CALORIES / 1G PROTEIN / 11G CARBS / 14G FAT / 0G DIETARY FIBRE PER SERVE

METHOD

1. Place the coconut sugar and water in a small saucepan. Cook over medium heat for 12–15 minutes, swirling the pan but not stirring. Do not let it bubble too rapidly or burn. When caramelized, it will have a strong caramel scent and dark amber colour.

2. Gently melt the cacao butter in a heat-proof bowl over a pan with a small amount of water on the stove, until all of the solids have dissolved.

3. While that is melting, blend the raw cashews in a blender until they are finely ground. (It's okay if it starts to turn into cashew butter!) Add in coconut sugar caramel, and blend again until very smooth. Once the cacao butter is completely melted, add to the cashew mixture and blend again until completely smooth.

4. Pour into the loaf pan, and smooth the top with a spatula. You'll notice that the mixture is more of an off-white/tan color when it's melted, but it will lighten up once it has set. It still won't be perfectly white, as is the nature of using all-natural ingredients, but the result is still pretty!

5. Place the pan in the freezer to set for 6 hours, or until very firm. Use a sharp knife to cut and serve the fudge chilled.

NOTES

- This fudge should remain solid at room temperature, but it will get significantly softer, so I recommend storing it in the freezer until ready to serve.

- 1/2 cup of cashew butter should equal 1 cup of raw cashews in most recipes. If you don't want to make your own cashew butter, I recommend Organic Road Cashew Butter (however it won't be classified as raw as the cashews have been roasted).

- For a festive variation, try making this a peppermint candy fudge, by adding 1/2 tsp of peppermint extract and sprinkling with Goji berries that have been pulsed in a blender or food processor for a few seconds.

Caramilk fudge & coffee catchup? x

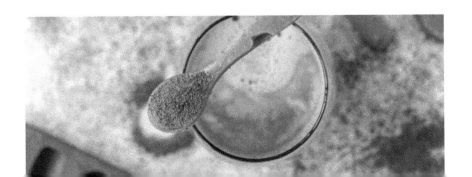

179

Ocean Smoothie Bowl

VEGAN | MAKES 1

Sunshiney weather has me dreaming of smoothie bowls like this one, inspired by the sea. There's only one smoothie bowl in this book, so rest assured this one is a goodie. *Drools*

INGREDIENTS

2 cups (200g) frozen pineapple

1/2 cup (90g) coconut or almond milk yoghurt

1 scoop (30g) vegan protein powder

1 tsp blue spirulina

Dash of water or coconut water

Optional fun toppings: white chocolate mermaid tails, toasted coconut flakes, chia seed pudding, melted peanut butter

METHOD

1. Process all ingredients in a blender until smooth and creamy.

NOTES

Optional to top with Salted Caramel Coconut Chips (page 198) and chia pudding!

NUTRITIONAL INFO

330 CALORIES / 21G PROTEIN / 31G CARBS / 11G FAT / 3G DIETARY FIBRE PER SERVE

Cookie Dough
Ice Cream Sandwiches

NO-BAKE | MAKES 8 SANDWICHES

No baking, no churning, no spoon required for this easy dessert recipe–these vegan and paleo cookie dough ice cream sandwiches are a healthy summer treat!

As for the micronutrients, dates and date paste are a good source of calcium, magnesium, and iron!

INGREDIENTS

Cookie Dough

1 cup dates, soaked in boiling water for 15 minutes, reserving the water

2/3 cup (80g) coconut flour *(Organic Road)*

1 tsp vanilla extract

Pinch of salt *(Natural Road)*

1/3 cup (60g) sugar-free chocolate chips*

Ice Cream *(or buy your own, but where's the fun in that?)*

3 frozen bananas

1 can full-fat coconut milk

NUTRITIONAL INFO

WITHOUT ICECREAM: 196 CALORIES / 5G PROTEIN / 30G CARBS / 7G FAT / 12G DIETARY FIBRE PER SERVE

METHOD

1. **COOKIE DOUGH:** Process soaked dates and 1/2 cup date water in the food processor until a smooth date paste. Combine all the cookie dough ingredients (except the choc chips) in the]processor until smooth. If it's dry, add a tiny bit of the date water. Stir through choc chips. Divide the dough in half. Press half of the dough firmly into of an 8×5" loaf pan lined with baking paper. Place in freezer to set while you make the ice cream or until it feels solid (about 10 minutes).

2. **ICE CREAM:** Blend the frozen bananas and coconut milk until smooth. Pour on top of the cookie dough. Freeze for 2 hours, stirring every 30 minutes to prevent ice crystals.

3. **ASSEMBLY:** Once the ice cream is firm enough, gently press the other half of the cookie dough on top on the ice cream. Freeze overnight (or at least 8 hours). Once frozen, slice into bars and enjoy! Store in the freezer for up to 3 months.

NOTES

*I use Well Naturally Sugar-Free Dark Choc

Kombucha, Watermelon & Mint Icy Poles

VEGAN | MAKES 6

INGREDIENTS

1 cup (250ml) kombucha (I like berry or ginger flavour)

1 1/2 cups (about 200g) watermelon, sliced into small cubes

1/2 bunch mint, leaves picked

NUTRITIONAL INFO

15 CALORIES / 0G PROTEIN / 0G CARBS / 0G FAT / 0G DIETARY FIBRE PER SERVE

METHOD

1. Equally divide and layer watermelon and mint in 6 icy pole molds.

2. Pour kombucha into each icy pole mould, stirring if necessary.

3. Cover with lids and freeze overnight or for 8 hours until completely set.

It's Mint to be..

No-Bake Blueberry & Lemon Cheesecake Pots

VEGAN OPTIONS | LOW CARB | MAKES 6 SERVES

INGREDIENTS

1 1/2 cups blueberries, fresh or frozen

2 tbsp powdered sweetener
(I process Organic Road Xylitol until it is a powdered form)

250g low fat cream cheese or vegan cream cheese

4 tbsp almond flour

zest of 1 lemon

NUTRITIONAL INFO

173 CALORIES / 1.3G PROTEIN / 14.7G CARBS / 12.9G FAT / 4G DIETARY FIBRE PER SERVE

METHOD

1. In a small pan bring to boil the blueberries and sweetener and cook over a fairly high heat for 5 minutes, stirring occasionally. Remove from the heat and leave to cool a little (about 10 min).

2. Process the blueberry mixture, cream cheese, almond flour and lemon zest until smooth.

3. Spoon equal amounts of the mixture into 4-5 pots or ramekins and refrigerate for at least 30 minutes before serving.

NOTES

You can swap out half of the cream cheese for non-fat Greek yoghurt to reduce calories.

Coconut Chia Pudding

VEGAN | SERVES 8

INGREDIENTS

1 can coconut milk *(Organic Road)*

1/2 cup chia seeds *(Organic Road)*

1–2 tbsp maple syrup *(more or less to taste)* *(Organic Road)*

1 tsp vanilla extract

Optional: 1 tsp blue spirulina and 1 tsp pink pitaya powder

NUTRITIONAL INFO

149 CALORIES / 3.3G PROTEIN /
9.5G CARBS / 11.3G FAT /
4.8G DIETARY FIBRE PER SERVE

METHOD

1. Whisk milk, chia seeds, maple syrup (to taste), and vanilla in a bowl. Cover and refrigerate overnight (or at least 6 hours). The chia pudding should be thick and creamy. If not, add more chia seeds, stir, and refrigerate for another hour or so.

2. Enjoy as is, or layer with compote or fresh fruit! Will keep covered in the refrigerator up to 5 days.

A chia-ful treat

Creamy Raw Vegan Dark Chocolate

VEGAN | SERVES 8

There's no better way to show someone how much they mean to you...than with chocolate! This velvety-rich raw vegan chocolate recipe is so versatile and the customizations are endless. I topped mine with freeze-dried strawberry and cacao nibs for extra crunch.

INGREDIENTS

1 cup (200g) raw cacao butter

3-5 tbsp liquid sweetener
(Maple Syrup, Agave, Honey etc)
(Organic Road)

1/2 cup (50g) raw cacao powder
(Organic Road)

1 tsp vanilla extract

1/4 tsp salt *(Natural Road)*

**Optional Mix-ins/Toppings:
roasted nuts, freeze-dried fruit,
cacao nibs.**

NUTRITIONAL INFO

133 CALORIES / 0.1G PROTEIN
/ 3.1G CARBS / 13.4G FAT / 0.1G
DIETARY FIBRE PER SERVE

METHOD

1. Set up a double-boiler by bringing 2 inches of water in a saucepan to a simmer over low heat. Then set a glass or ceramic bowl on top, making sure it doesn't touch the water.

2. Add cacao butter and melt for a few minutes. To keep raw, do not let ingredients heat to above 40°C/104°F.

3. Whisk in the sweetener, cacao powder, vanilla and salt until combined and very smooth. Turn off heat.

4. Taste and adjust flavour/sweetener as needed. Add mix-ins if desired.

5. Choose your chocolate mould – cupcake liners, chocolate bar moulds etc – and carefully pour in the chocolate. Set in the freezer or refrigerator, about 10 minutes. Store in freezer for up to one month.

Salted Caramel Chocolate Icecream

HIGH-PROTEIN | VEGAN | MAKES 20 SERVES

INGREDIENTS

3 cups (390g) pitted dates
(if not sticky and moist, soak in hot water for 10 minutes)

2 cans coconut cream or full-fat coconut milk, chilled overnight in the fridge *(Organic Road)*

2/3 cup (50g) raw cacao powder *(Organic Road)*

1/3 (35g) vegan protein powder

1 tsp vanilla extract

OPTIONAL MIX-INS

Pinch of salt for salted caramel flavour *(Natural Road)*

1 tbsp instant coffee powder

1/2 tsp cinnamon

Cacao nibs or choc chips

NUTRITIONAL INFO

100 CALORIES / 1.4G PROTEIN / 11.9G CARBS / 5.7G FAT / 1.1G DIETARY FIBRE PER SERVE

METHOD

1. Place a large mixing bowl in the freezer to chill for 10 minutes.

2. In the meantime, add the moist, pitted dates to a food processor and process until small bits remain. Then add a bit of the date water a little at a time until it forms a thick, creamy paste. Scoop out half of the date paste in a bowl and set aside.

3. Scoop out the creamy part ONLY of the coconut cans into the food processor, reserving 1/2 cup of the liquid in the can. NOTE: If you're using coconut milk, you'll likely use less sweetener because there's less volume. Process until smooth.

4. Then process cocoa powder, protein powder, vanilla, coconut liquid until smooth.

5. Taste and adjust flavors as needed. I ended up adding most of the date paste. Transfer to a lined freezer-safe container and cover loosely with plastic wrap, then foil to help freeze.

6. Remove container in a couple of hours for a chilled mousse-like ice cream. Freeze overnight for a firmer ice cream. Set out for at least 20 minutes prior to scooping. Will keep in the freezer for up to one week, but best when fresh.

193

Jazz it up!

Pitaya, Lime & Chia Dip

VEGAN | RAW | 15 SERVES

This sweet dip is perfect for jazzing up your fruit and serving up an easy but unique party platter that'll be sure to impress your guests.

INGREDIENTS

1 can of full fat coconut milk or cream *(refrigerated overnight)* *(Organic Road)*

3 tbsp chia seeds *(Organic Road)*

2 tbsp sweetener of choice *(maple syrup, coconut sugar, agave, etc)* *(Organic Road)*

1 tbsp pitaya powder

½ tsp vanilla extract

½ lime, squeezed

METHOD

1. Scrape the creamy part of the canned coconut milk that has risen to the top, reserving or discarding the leftover water.

2. Mix all ingredients together and refrigerate for a few minutes to thicken.

NUTRITIONAL INFO

59 CALORIES / 1G PROTEIN / 3.7G CARBS / 4.6G FAT / 1G DIETARY FIBRE PER SERVE

Snacks

Salted Caramel Coconut Chips

PALEO | VEGAN | GLUTEN-FREE | DAIRY-FREE | REFINED SUGAR-FREE | MAKES 10 SERVES (2 CUPS TOTAL)

Warning: DANGEROUSLY ADDICTIVE. Crispy, sweet 'n' salty coconut chips caramelized to perfection. Be careful not to eat it all at once, I've made these countless times...and never shared. They'd make a cute gift for a loved one in an airtight mason jar.

INGREDIENTS

1 1/2 tbsp (15g) coconut sugar
(Organic Road)

1/4 tsp salt *(Natural Road)*

1 tbsp warm water

1 1/2 cups (65g) coconut flakes
(Organic Road)

NUTRITIONAL INFO

38 CALORIES / 0G PROTEIN /
5G CARBS / 2G FAT /
0G DIETARY FIBRE

METHOD

1. Preheat the oven to 150°C/300°F fan-forced. Line a baking tray.

2. In a large bowl, whisk together coconut sugar, salt and water until sugar is dissolved, about 1–2 minutes. Stir in coconut until it is well-coated in sugar mixture.

3. Pour mixture onto the prepared baking tray, spreading into an even, thin layer, creating empty pockets for air to flow though while baking. Bake for 10 minutes. Stir and flip the coconut chips. Bake for an additional 4–8 minutes, watching closely until they're thoroughly toasted and dried out - be careful as they burn easily! Chips are soft when you remove them, but will crisp up when cool. Store in an airtight container for 1 month at room temperature in a cool, dark environment.

NOTES

If the chips soften (usually due to heat exposure), place in the refrigerator to crisp up. You may store these in the refrigerator for up to a month - if you don't eat them all! Freezer for 3 months.

Dangerously addictive

199

Almond Salted Caramel Fudge

PALEO | VEGAN | MAKES 20 BITE SIZED SERVES

Creamy 3 ingredient nut butter fudge that's healthy, easy, and has a luscious "pull apart" (like caramel!)! Silky smooth, and easy to make, it's a party pleaser.

INGREDIENTS

3/4 cup (380g) almond or cashew butter *(Organic Road)*

1/2 cup (170g) maple syrup *(Organic Road)*

2 tbsp (20g) coconut oil *(Organic Road)*

1 tsp vanilla extract

sea salt flakes for topping

NUTRITIONAL INFO

144 CALORIES / 2G PROTEIN / 11G CARBS / 10G FAT / 0G DIETARY FIBRE

METHOD

1. In a food processor, blend all ingredients (except the salt) until completely smooth.

2. Line a 4" by 4" square cake pan with baking paper. Pour the cashew butter into the cake pan and freeze for 1 hour or until solid.

3. Sprinkle with sea salt flakes, cut, and serve or store in the freezer for optimum freshness.

NOTES

For this recipe it is best to use a 4" by 4" square cake pan, but a bread pan will also work.

Pecan Pie

VEGAN | PROTEIN | SERVES 10

Pecan pie is the perfect combination of sweet, gooey and nutty. However, the store-bought version is full of white sugar, preservatives, refined flour and rancid oils. This clean, crowd-pleasing Pecan Pie that's easy, fast, delicious and requires no baking! It only requires 4 simple ingredients that you probably already have in your pantry, so you literally have no excuses not to give this a go. One of my favourite raw treats in this book!

INGREDIENTS

Crust

1 and 1/2 cup (150g) pecans *(or other nut of choice; cashews, walnuts or almonds work well)*

3/4 cup (60g) desiccated coconut *(Organic Road)*

1/4 cup (30g) vanilla protein powder *(or substitute for more coconut) (Organic Road)*

4 dates (96g), pitted and chopped

1 tbsp water

Filling

6 dates (144g) dates, pitted and chopped

3/4 cup water

1/2 cup (50g) pecans, roughly chopped

1/2 cup (60g) vanilla protein powder *(optional; you can also omit completely) (Organic Road)*

1/4 tsp salt *(Natural Road)*

METHOD

1. **CRUST:** Add all crust ingredients to a food processor and process until crumbled. Press crust mixture evenly into a lined pie dish (I used a circle dish 7 inches in diameter) and place in the freezer to firm up whilst you prepare the filling.

2. **FILLING:** Place the chopped dates in a saucepan and cover with water. Bring to a boil, then reduce heat to simmer until a thick gooey mixture forms (about 10-15 minutes). Add more water if necessary.

3. Stir in the protein powder and salt evenly, then stir in the pecans. Remove from heat and let it cool.

4. **ASSEMBLY:** Take the crust out of the freezer and pour the filling on top. Decorate with more pecans if desired and place in the freezer for 30 minutes or the fridge for 2 hours to firm up. Enjoy and store leftovers in the fridge or freezer.

NUTRITIONAL INFO

120 CALORIES / 5G PROTEIN / 22G CARBS / 19G FAT / 5G DIETARY FIBRE PER SERVE

Peanut Butter & Jelly Protein Balls

VEGAN | HIGH-PROTEIN | MAKES 8 BALLS

The perfect portable protein snack for before or after your workout, with the delicious flavour of peanut butter and berry jam..

INGREDIENTS

1 cup (115g) oat flour
(Organic Road Rolled Oats processed into flour)

1/4 cup (30g) vegan protein powder

1/2 cup (125g) peanut butter

1/4 cup (85g) maple syrup
(Organic Road)

1/4 cup water

1/4 cup store-bought strawberry jam or berry chia jam on page 228

METHOD

1. Mix all ingredients into a bowl or food processor, until the mixture clumps like cookie dough.

2. Divide the mixture into 8 balls, and roll into a ball and flatten. Place a teaspoon of jam in the centre before moulding into ball shapes.

3. Freeze for 30 mins to firm up the protein balls, and optional to drizzle with some extra peanut butter! Store in an airtight container in refrigerator for about 2 weeks, or freezer for 3 months.

NUTRITIONAL INFO

229 CALORIES / 8.2G PROTEIN / 30.3G CARBS / 9G FAT / 2.4G DIETARY FIBRE PER BALL

Perfect protein snack

Salted Caramel Macadamia Cups

VEGAN | MAKES 10

INGREDIENTS

Base

3/4 cup (90g) macadamias, roasted

1 cup (100g) rolled oats
(Organic Road)

1 cup (90g) desiccated coconut
(Organic Road)

5 medjool dates, pitted

1 tbsp coconut oil, melted
(Organic Road)

Filling

10 medjool dates, pitted

1/2 cup water

1/2 tsp salt *(Natural Road)*

Optional:

 ~30 whole roasted macadamias

1/2 cup (75g) chocolate, gently melted *(I use Well Naturally Salted Caramel chocolate)*

NUTRITIONAL INFO

236 CALORIES / 3G PROTEIN / 34G CARBS / 12G FAT / 5G DIETARY FIBRE PER SERVE

METHOD

1. **BASE:** Combine all of the base ingredients into a food processor. Process until it becomes smooth and sticky. Press the mixture into the base of 9 muffin moulds. Use your fingers to press the mixture up against the edges to form a bowl or cup shape. Place in freezer to set while you make filling.

2. **FILLING:** Add all the filling ingredients to the processor and blend until smooth and thick.

3. **ASSEMBLY:** Spoon the mixture evenly into each of the cups, shaking to even out. Optional to press macadamias into each cup. Return to freezer. Optional: melt chocolate gently on a low heat in the microwave and drizzle over cups and return to freezer. Remove the base from the tray by sliding a small sharp knife to lift the cup out. Transfer to a container and store in the freezer for up to 2 weeks.

Jaffa Truffles

GLUTEN FREE | VEGAN | MAKES 10 TRUFFLES

INGREDIENTS

220g dates, pitted 200g

1/3 cup (25g) desiccated coconut
(Organic Road)

1/4 cup (25g) almond meal

2 tsp orange rind, finely grated

1 1/2 tbsp (15g) cacao powder
(Organic Road)

NUTRITIONAL INFO

97 CALORIES / 1.5G PROTEIN
/ 18.6G CARBS / 3.2G FAT / 3
DIETARY FIBRE PER TRUFFLE

METHOD

1. Process dates until it becomes date paste, if the dates are not moist, soak in boiling water for 15 minutes first. Add the soaked date water if necessary until it is a paste texture.

2. Add all other ingredients until mixture is combined and starts to clump.

3. Roll mixture into 10 balls. Optional: roll balls in extra cocoa powde or melted chocolate. Place in fridge for 20 minutes until firm. Store truffles in airtight container for two weeks.

Cacao Hemp Protein Balls

GLUTEN FREE | FLOURLESS | MAKES 16 TRUFFLES

INGREDIENTS

1 packed cup (130g) dates, pitted

1/4 cup (25g) hemp seeds, plus extra for topping *(13 Seeds)*

3 tbsp (21g) cacao powder *(Organic Road)*

1 cup (110g) roasted almonds or walnuts

3/4 cup (130g) sugar-free dark chocolate *(Well Naturally)*

METHOD

1. Place dates, hemp seeds, cacao powder, and almonds (reserving 16) in food processor. Blend until well combined.

2. Roll a tablespoon of mixture into a ball and poke an almond in the middle. Mould mixture into a ball around nut. Repeat with remaining mixture.

NUTRITIONAL INFO

WITH DARK CHOCOLATE: 180 CALORIES / 5.3G PROTEIN / 24.5G CARBS / 9.9G FAT / 4.5 DIETARY FIBRE PER TRUFFLE

WITHOUT DARK CHOCOLATE: 138 CALORIES / 4.7G PROTEIN / 18.5G CARBS / 7.5G FAT / 4.5 DIETARY FIBRE PER TRUFFLE

Chocolate Crackle Bliss Balls

MAKES 14 SERVES

INGREDIENTS

1/2 cup (120g) hulled tahini
(Organic Road)

1/3 cup (115g) honey
(Organic Road)

1/4 cup (30g) cacao powder
(Organic Road)

1 tsp vanilla extract

1/4 tsp salt *(Natural Road)*

2 cups (48g) corn thins, crushed
(Corn Thins Wholegrain)

1/2 cup (45g) desiccated coconut or ground flaxseed
(Organic Road)

Optional: mixed dried berries

NUTRITIONAL INFO

133 CALORIES / 3G PROTEIN / 12G CARBS / 8G FAT / 2G DIETARY FIBRE PER SERVE

METHOD

1. Place the tahini and honey into a bowl and mix to combine.

2. Mix in the cacao, vanilla and salt until combined. Add the remaining ingredients and mix to combine. Use your hands to press and shape the mixture into balls, place the balls in the fridge to set.

TIPS

- You may find it easiest to roll the balls with slightly damp hands or hands dusted with cacao.

- For a naturally festive-coloured dessert, use red and green fruit and nuts - such as pepitas, pistachios, goji berries and cranberries.

Raw Carrot Cake Bliss Balls

VEGAN | PROTEIN | MAKES 16 BALLS

These balls of goodness are the healthier alternative to a traditional carrot cake. They have all the flavour of your favourite carrot cake and can be prepared in a fraction of the time. Add hemp seeds to anything and everything to boost the protein and essential fatty acids.

INGREDIENTS

3/4 cup hemp seeds *(13 Seeds)*

1 cup (100g) shredded coconut *(Organic Road)*

½ tsp cinnamon *(Organic Road)*

½ tsp salt *(Natural Road)*

12 soft Medjool dates, pitted and soaked if they're dry

2/3 cup carrots, chopped or grated

Optional 1 tbsp maple syrup or more to taste *(Organic Road)*

Optional: 1/3 cup desiccated coconut for rolling, 1/4 cup melted white chocolate for decorating

NUTRITIONAL INFO

148 CALORIES / 3G PROTEIN / 14G CARBS / 10G FAT / 2G DIETARY FIBRE PER SERVE

METHOD

1. In a food processor, combine the sunflower seeds, 1 cup shredded coconut, cinnamon and salt and pulse until it becomes a fine meal.

2. Add the dates and carrots and pulse until the mixture combines and sticks together. Taste and add maple syrup if you would like your balls sweeter. If the mixture is too dry, add a tiny bit of water, if it's too moist, add more coconut and/or let the mix chill in the fridge for 20 minutes to firm up.

3. Use a tablespoon to scoop the mixture, then use your hands to roll it into approximately 1-inch balls.

4. Roll in the desiccated coconut and drizzle melted white chocolate if desired. Store in the fridge in an airtight container for up to 5 days.

Super soft,
fluffy, and
spring-y!

Vegan Vanilla Donuts

GLUTEN-FREE | VEGAN | MAKES 12 DONUTS

*These super soft, fluffy, and spring-y Vegan Vanilla Donuts
make the perfect base for getting creative with your toppings...
I use a variety of antioxidant rich berries, nuts and seeds,
buckinis, desiccated coconut. YUM!*

INGREDIENTS

1 1/2 cup (200g) gluten-free self raising flour *(if not self raising add 1 tsp baking powder)*

2 tbsp maple syrup or xylitol for sugar-free *(Organic Road)*

2 tbsp (20g) olive or coconut oil, melted *(Organic Road)*

1/2 cup (120g) almond milk

1 tbsp vanilla essence

Pinch salt *(Natural Road)*

Optional topping: sugar-free chocolate, melted *(Well Naturally)*

NUTRITIONAL INFO

WITHOUT GLAZE: 65 CALORIES / 1G PROTEIN / 11G CARBS / 2G FAT / 0G DIETARY FIBRE PER SERVE

WITH GLAZE: 88 CALORIES / 1G PROTEIN / 16G CARBS / 2G FAT / 0G DIETARY FIBRE PER SERVE

METHOD

1. Preheat your oven to 180°C/360°F

2. In a large mixing bowl mix together the gluten free flour, maple syrup, coconut oil and milk until it is a smooth batter.

3. Grease your doughnut mould lightly with coconut oil and add the batter into each mould making sure to smooth over the top

4. Add to the oven for 12-15 minutes (depending how hot your oven runs). Let cool for 10 minutes before adding any toppings.

NOTES

Optional Vanilla Glaze

- 1/2 cup powdered sweetener (for sugar-free, blend xylitol until it's a powdered form)
- 2 tsp vanilla extract
- 3 tsp water

METHOD

1. Mix the sweetenr vanilla and water together to create a thin glaze.
2. Use a large slotted spoon to drizzle the glaze over the donuts.
3. Allow the glaze to harden for several minutes before serving.
4. red and green fruit and nuts - such as pepitas, pistachios, goji berries and cranberries.

Grilled Banana Split

VEGAN | MAKES 2

INGREDIENTS

2 bananas halved lengthwise, skins kept on

1 tbsp (20g) coconut sugar
(Organic Road)

OPTIONAL TO SERVE

Coconut whipped cream on page 232

Salted caramel sauce on page 236

Chopped roasted peanuts

Vanilla ice cream

Fresh strawberries

NUTRITIONAL INFO

150 CALORIES / 1G PROTEIN / 39G CARBS / 0G FAT / 3G DIETARY FIBRE PER SERVE

METHOD

1. Sprinkle coconut sugar on the cut side of the bananas, then press the cut side down over a grill pan until they start to soften and caramelize. The sugar will burn quickly so keep a close eye on them. When the bananas are grilled, serve with scoops of vanilla ice cream and whipped cream, drizzle with the hot fudge and add the strawberries and cherries.
Serve immediately.

Honey Roasted Nuts

VEGAN OPTIONS | MAKES 4 CUPS/18 SERVINGS

Tasty, easy and healthy snack, what more could you ask for?! Perfect for popping into a glass jar for parties and cute gifts too!

INGREDIENTS

4 cups nuts/seeds (*I used half macadamia, half walnut and some hemp seeds*) (*13 Seeds*)

1 cup honey or maple syrup for vegan (*Organic Road*)

Optional: 4 tbsp butter or vegan butter for vegan

1 tsp cinnamon (*Organic Road*)

AFTER BAKING

1 tsp cinnamon (*Organic Road*)

4 tbsp coconut sugar (*Organic Road*)

1 1/2 tsp salt (*Natural Road*)

NUTRITIONAL INFO

MACADAMIA NUTS: 267 CALORIES / 2G PROTEIN / 22G CARBS / 21G FAT / 3G DIETARY FIBRE PER SERVE

METHOD

1. Preheat oven to 160°C/320°F.

2. In a small saucepan over medium heat, stir the honey, butter, cinnamon until melted. Once it starts to bubble, keep stirring for about 2 minutes. Stir through the nuts until evenly coated.

3. Pour the nuts onto 2 large baking trays, ensuring the nuts are spread out as much as possible so they all get an even browning in the oven. Bake in the oven for 20 minutes.

4. Half way through the baking, or when you see the nuts start to turn golden brown, use a spatula and turn the nuts over and return to the oven for the remaining bake time. When the time is up, check for a nice golden brown like in the photos. If the nuts need a bit longer in the oven just pop them back in but keep an eye out they don't burn!

5. Once done, remove from the oven and let sit to cool for about 15 minutes. Then transfer the nuts to a mixing bowl and add the coconut sugar and cinnamon, together with the salt.

6. Turn the nuts out back to the tray and spread out so they are not clumped together. Allow to cool until they are not sticky. Depending on the temperature, it should take around 1 - 3 hours for them to completely cool and dry out. Store in an airtight container or package in some nice jars to give as gifts.

Oil-Free Popcorn 3 Ways

VEGAN | 4 SERVES

"Is popcorn healthy?" I hear you ask. In the crunchy, salty snacks category, popcorn is definitely one of the healthier options. You can enjoy a large serving (2 1/2 cups) of popcorn for the same amount of calories as a handful of corn chips.

INGREDIENTS

½ a cup popcorn kernels
(amount can be less or more depending on your pot - as the kernels must be placed in one layer in the pot)

NUTRITIONAL INFO

7 CALORIES / 0G PROTEIN / 1G CARBS / 0G FAT / 0G DIETARY FIBRE PER SERVE

METHOD

1. Place the popcorn kernels in one layer on the bottom of a deep pot, as shown in the picture in the post above, and close with the lid

2. Turn on stove on medium heat

3. Stay close to the stove as you'll need to listen to the kernels as they pop. At the beginning the popcorn will pop vigorously. When there is an interval of a second or two between the pop sounds this is the time to turn the stove off

4. Wait a few minutes for the popcorn to cool and move it to your desired bowl

NOTES

If you wish, you can add 1 tbsp of coconut or olive oil to the pan.

VARIATIONS

Matcha (Green Tea) Popcorn

- Stir together 1 tsp matcha powder + 3/4 cup white chocolate, melted. Stir through popcorn.

Salted Caramel Popcorn

- 1/2 cup salted caramel sauce on page _. Stir through popcorn.

Berry Cheesecake Protein Pizza

HIGH-PROTEIN | MAKES 10 SLICES

INGREDIENTS

PIZZA DOUGH

1 cup nonfat plain greek yoghurt (220g)

1 cup self-rising flour (150g)

TOPPING

225g low fat cream cheese
(regular or vegan)

1 scoop (30g) protein of choice
(Natural Road)

Optional: 2-3 tbsp (60g) sweetener, to taste
(honey, maple syrup etc)
(Organic Road)

Optional 1/2 tsp lemon zest, finely grated

2-4 tbsp water

3-4 cups mixed berries

NUTRITIONAL INFO

135 CALORIES / 5G PROTEIN / 17G CARBS / 6G FAT / 2G DIETARY FIBRE PER SERVE

METHOD

PIZZA BASE:

1. Preheat Oven to 180°C/

2. Stir Together yoghurt and flour until a tick dough forms.

3. Knead dough on a lightly floured surface until it forms a dough ball.

4. Place dough ball on a sheet of baking paper. Roll out to desired size (approximately 10-inches diameter). Place on a baking tray or pizza pan/stone.

5. Bake for 20 minutes, or until golden brown and cooked through.

CHEESECAKE FILLING:

1. Beat softened cream cheese in a mixing bowl food processor until smooth.

2. Add protein, sweetener, lemon and add 1tbsp of water at a time, until mixture is creamy and spreads easily with the spatula.

3. Taste and adjust sweetness as needed.

TOPPING:

1. Prepare berries i.e. slice strawberries and large blackberries in half.

2. Place half the berries onto the pizza dough and top with cheesecake filling, then scatter the remaining berries over the cheesecake filling.

3. Bake in preheated oven for another 10-15 minutes.

4. Remove from the oven and let cool slightly before slicing.

Sweet
Sides

Berry Chia Jam

VEGAN | MAKES 10 SERVES

This Easy 3-Ingredient Chia Seed Strawberry Jam is the perfect healthy alternative to conventional jam! It's made with 3 healthy, natural, whole-food ingredients and it's quick and easy to make! It's the perfect use for overripe fruit and the chia seeds will not only give the jam a gelatinous texture, it will also add fibre, protein and healthy Omega-3 fats. I love using this jam for the Coco Vanilla & Jam Tea Cake on page 121.

INGREDIENTS

450g frozen or fresh mixed berries of choice, *(blueberries, raspberries, strawberries)* **washed, hulled, and sliced**

3 tbsp maple syrup or honey *(add 1 more tablespoon if you like your jam very sweet)* *(Organic Road)*

2 tbsp chia seeds *(Organic Road)*

NUTRITIONAL INFO

48 CALORIES / 1G PROTEIN / 9G CARBS / 1G FAT / 2G DIETARY FIBRE PER SERVE

METHOD

1. Heat a medium saucepan over medium heat and add the berries. Add the sweetener of choice and place on the stove over medium heat.

2. As the berries begin to soften over the heat, stir them around in their juices. Once the berries have softened to the point that they're starting to fall apart, use a fork to break them up even more.

3. Let the mixture come to a slow boil, stirring almost continually. Once you see some big bubbles break the surface, add the chia seeds which will help the jam achieve a gelatinous texture while also adding fibre, protein and healthy Omega-3 fats. Continue stirring the mixture over low heat for about 15 minutes, and then remove the pan from the stove.

4. If you enjoy jam slightly chunky, then you're done! Simply pour the mixture into a mason jar and cover it tightly with a lid. For a smoother texture, feel free to add the mixture to your blender and pulse it a few times before pouring it into a jar.

NOTES

While the jam is still hot it may seem more fluid that you would expect. The chia seeds need a bit of time to do their work, so put your jar of jam in the fridge for a few hours and it will achieve the perfect texture. It keeps for about 1-2 weeks in the fridge, as it has no preservatives.

Enjoy on toast, gluten-free crackers or scones, over yogurt or even ice cream on page 192

Healthy Nutella

VEGAN | MAKES 10 SERVES

Everyone needs a healthy Nutella in their recipe arsenal and this healthified version of everyone's favourite chocolate hazelnut spread is as easy as it gets!

INGREDIENTS

3 cups hazelnuts, roasted, unsalted, skins removed

1 tsp vanilla extract

1/2 tsp salt *(Natural Road)*

2/3 cup (130g) vegan dark chocolate or sugar-free dark chocolate, melted

METHOD

1. Blend hazelnuts in a food processor or high-speed blender until a smooth, creamy butter is formed – about 8-10 minutes total – scraping down sides as needed.

2. Add the vanilla and salt to the hazelnut butter and blend well. Then slowly add melted chocolate and blend again until thoroughly mixed. Taste and adjust seasonings as needed, adding more salt or vanilla if desired.

NUTRITIONAL INFO

59 CALORIES / 0.4G PROTEIN / 4.3G CARBS / 4G FAT / 1.7G DIETARY FIBRE PER SERVE

You had me
at Nutella

Coconut Whipped Cream

VEGAN | MAKES 10 SERVINGS

*Cold coconut milk, cold beaters and a cold mixing bowl are the
only tricks you need to make vegan whipped cream. Keep one
or two tins of coconut milk in your fridge so that you're always
ready to make this recipe! Experiment with additions like
citrus zest, matcha (green tea) powder, cocoa powder, almond
extract, and more! I love using this as frosting for my Coco
Vanilla & Jam Tea Cake on page 121*

INGREDIENTS

**1 (400ml) can coconut milk or
coconut cream is even better**
(Organic Road)

**2 tbsp powdered sweetener, or
to taste** *(I process Organic Road
Xylitol until it's a powdered form)*

1 tsp vanilla extract

METHOD

1. Chill canned coconut milk in the fridge for 8 hours or overnight.

2. Place metal mixing bowl and whisk in the fridge or freezer 1 hour before making the whipped cream.

3. Open tin of coconut milk, the coconut cream will have solidified and separated from the milk. Scoop out the solid coconut cream into the cold mixing bowl. Reserve the liquid coconut milk for another use, such as a smoothie.

4. Beat coconut cream using electric mixer with chilled beaters on medium speed; increase to high speed. Beat until stiff peaks form, 7 to 8 minutes. Add sugar and vanilla extract to coconut cream; beat 1 minute more. Taste and add more sugar if desired.

NOTES

You MUST use an electric mixer – for another coconut frosting recipe without an electric mixer, try the Coconut "Buttercream" recipe on page 233

NUTRITIONAL INFO

24CALORIES / 0G PROTEIN /
4G CARBS / 1G FAT / 0G DIETARY
FIBRE PER SERVE

Coconut "Buttercream" Frosting

VEGAN | MAKES 3 CUPS OR 10 SERVINGS

There's nothing better than the icing on top of a cake, and this Coconut "Buttercream" Frosting is evidence of this! It's a made from scratch, simple recipe that is perfect slathered on cakes, cupcakes, or right from the spoon. I love using this as frosting for my Coco Vanilla & Jam Sponge Cake on page 121 if you don't have an electic mixer for the Coconut whipped cream recipe.

INGREDIENTS

3/4 cups (150g) vegan butter, softened

2 1/2 cups (300g) powdered sugar *(I process coconut sugar or xylitol for sugar-free until it's powdered form) (Organic Road)*

3 tbsp corn or tapioca starch

1/8 tsp salt *(Natural Road)*

6 tbsp canned coconut milk or coconut cream is even better *(Organic Road)*

1 tsp vanilla extract

NUTRITIONAL INFO

186 CALORIES / 0G PROTEIN / 32G CARBS / 12G FAT / 0G DIETARY FIBRE PER SERVE

METHOD

1. Using a handheld mixer mixer fitted with the paddle attachment, beat the butter on medium-high speed until smooth and creamy, about 5 minutes. You can use a food processor but the result will not be as whipped and airy, but it still tastes lovely!

2. Add powdered sugar, beat on medium-low speed until most of the sugar is moistened. Gradually add in the remaining sugar, mixing well after each addition. Stop to scrape down the sides of the bowl as needed.

3. And the salt, coconut milk and vanilla, beating on medium speed until fully incorporated. You may need more or less of the coconut milk depending on how strong you'd like the flavor.

4. Turn the speed up to medium-high and beat until light and fluffy. Scrape down the sides of the bowl as needed. Taste test and make any adjustments as desired. Frosting will keep for up to 4 days stored in the refrigerator in an airtight container. Let stand at room temperature to soften before use.

5. Or it can be frozen for up to 3 months. When ready to use, place in the refrigerator overnight to thaw. Let stand at room temperature to soften before use.

NOTES

- Soften the butter by allowing it to sit at room temperature for 1-2 hours prior to making the frosting. DO NOT soften the butter by heating it in the microwave!

- It is important to shake the can of coconut milk/cream vigorously before opening it. The fats and liquids separate in the can after sitting. You want a combination of both for the frosting, so mix it very well.

- If the coconut flavor isn't as strong as you'd like, try adding 1/2 to 1 teaspoon coconut extract.

Hemp Seed "Butter"

VEGAN | MAKES 8 SERVES

INGREDIENTS

80g hemp seeds *(13 Seeds)*

3 tbsp (30g) coconut oil + extra, if needed *(Organic Road)*

2 dates, pitted

Optional: maple syrup, to sweeten *(Organic Road)*

NUTRITIONAL INFO

119 CALORIES / 3G PROTEIN / 5G CARBS / 9G FAT / 0G DIETARY FIBRE PER SERVE

METHOD

1. Place all the ingredients in the bowl of a stick blender and mix on high speed until a thick butter is formed. Add a little more coconut oil for a smoother texture, if needed.

2. Taste and add more maple syrup to sweeten, if desired.

I like you butter than anyone

Crazy for Caramel

All of these Caramels are deliciously salty 'n' sweet and go perfectly with so many desserts - let your imagination go wild! Pick the one that has the ingredients you vibe with. They a perfect match for Oil-Free Popcorn (page 222), Grilled Banana Split (page 219), drizzled over the Chocolate Protein Icecream on page 192, a topping brownies and cakes, the options are truly endless.

Coconut Sugar Caramel Sauce

VEGAN | MAKES 10 SERVES

INGREDIENTS

1 cup coconut sugar
(Organic Road)

1/4 cup water

2/3 cup coconut cream
(Organic Road)

1/2 tsp vanilla extract

1/4 tsp salt *(Natural Road)*

NUTRITIONAL INFO

99 CALORIES / 0G PROTEIN / 20G CARBS / 3G FAT / 0G DIETARY FIBRE PER SERVE

METHOD

1. Heat the coconut sugar and water in a small saucepan. Cook over medium heat for 12-15 minutes, swirling the pan but not stirring. Reduce heat slighlty if mixture is bubbling too rapidly. And remove it from heat if it begins smelling burnt. When caramelized, it will have a strong caramel scent and dark amber colour.

2. Once caramelized remove from heat and whisk in coconut cream, vanilla and salt. Let cool, then transfer to a lidded jar. Store in fridge for 2-3 weeks. Reheat in microwave, or it's just as delicious served chilled over your favourite icecream or dessert.

Peanut Butter Caramel Sauce

VEGAN | MAKES 10 SERVES

The easiest, dreamiest and creamiest peanut butter caramel, that only takes a few minutes to prepare. Use it on pancakes, ice cream, brownies or whatever your heart desires!

INGREDIENTS

1/2 cup (170g) maple syrup
(Organic Road)

1/4 cup (60g) peanut butter *(add 1/4 tsp salt if no salt is added)*

1/2 tsp vanilla extract

NUTRITIONAL INFO

56 CALORIES / 0G PROTEIN / 12G CARBS / 1G FAT / 0G DIETARY FIBRE PER SERVE

METHOD

1. In a small saucepan, whisk all of the ingredients well until smooth, and bring to a boil. Whisk continuously for about a minute or so until it starts to thicken up. That's it! It happens quickly. Keep in mind, the longer you cook it, the thicker it will get, and it will thicken up a lot as it cools as well. If you want to thin it out, add a little water to desired thickness.

TIPS

If using almond butter instead of peanut butter it will take a little bit longer to thicken up.

1 Ingredient Date Caramel

VEGAN | MAKES 4 SERVES

INGREDIENTS

20 large pitted dates *(if not moist and sticky, soak in hot water for 10 minutes, reserving the date water)*

1/4 salt (optional) *(Natural Road)*

NUTRITIONAL INFO

266 CALORIES / 2G PROTEIN / 72G CARBS / 0G FAT / 6G DIETARY FIBRE PER SERVE

METHOD

1. Add pitted dates to a food processor (best) or high-speed blender.

2. Pulse/mix on low until small bits remain. Then stream in hot water while the processor is on until a paste is made. You will need to scrape the down sides periodically. Add a pinch of salt.

3. Be sure to only add enough water to form a paste – too much and it will be too liquidy. Amount will depend on your machine and size/moistness of dates. Keep refrigerated in airtight jar for 1-2 weeks.

TIPS

It's also the perfect sweetener for your morning oats or smoothies.

Superfood Sprinkles

VEGAN | MAKES 5

INGREDIENTS

1 cup desiccated coconut or shredded coconut *(Organic Road)*

Pink: 1 tsp pitaya *(pink dragonfruit)* **powder**

Blue: 1 tsp blue spirulina

Green: 1 tsp matcha powder

Yellow: 1 tsp turmeric

NUTRITIONAL INFO

55 CALORIES / 1G PROTEIN / 1G CARBS / 5G FAT / 2G DIETARY FIBRE PER SERVE

METHOD

1. Divide coconut into 5 small bowls

2. Add the colouring into each bowl and stir until combined

Life is better with sprinkles

Measurement Conversions

One Australian metric measuring cup holds approximately 250ml; one Australian metric tablespoon holds 20ml; one Australian metric teaspoon holds 5ml

The difference between one country's measuring cups and another's is within a two or three teaspoon variance and will not affect your cooking results. North America, New Zealand and the United Kingdom use a 15ml tablespoon.

All cup and spoon measurements are level. The most accurate way of measuring dry ingredients is to weigh them. When measuring liquids, use a clear glass or plastic jug with the metric markings.

The imperial measurements used in these recipes are approximate only. Measurements for cake pans are approximate only. Using same-shaped cake pans of a similar size should not affect the outcome of your baking. We measure the inside top of the cake pan to determine size.

We use large eggs with an average weight of 60g.

Dry measures	
Metric	Imperial
15g	½ OZ
30g	1OZ
60g	2OZ
90g	3OZ
125g	4OZ
155g	5OZ
185g	6OZ
220g	7OZ
250g	8OZ
280g	9OZ
315g	10OZ
345g	11OZ
375g	12OZ
410g	13OZ
440g	14OZ
470g	15OZ
500g	16OZ (1LB)
750g	24OZ (1 ½ LB)
1kg	32OZ (2LB)

Liquid measures	
Metric	Imperial
30ml	1 Fluid OZ
60ml	2 Fluid OZ
100ml	3 Fluid OZ
125ml	4 Fluid OZ
150ml	5 Fluid OZ
190ml	6 Fluid OZ
250ml	8 Fluid OZ
300ml	10 Fluid OZ
500ml	16 Fluid OZ
600ml	20 Fluid OZ
1000ml (1 Litre)	1 ¾ pints

Length Measures

Metric	Imperial
3mm	⅛ in
6mm	¼ in
1cm	½ in
2cm	¾ in
2.5cm	1 in
5cm	2 in
6cm	2 ½ in
8cm	3 in
10cm	4 in
13cm	5 in
15cm	6 in
18cm	7 in
20cm	8 in
22cm	9 in
25cm	10 in
28cm	11 in
30cm	12 in (1ft)

Oven Temperatures

The oven temperatures in this book are for conventional ovens; if you have a fan-forced oven, decrease the temperature by 10-20 degrees

	°C (Celsius)	°F (Farenheit)
Very slow	120	250
Slow	150	300
Moderately slow	160	325
Moderate	180	350
Moderately hot	200	400
Hot	220	425
Very hot	240	475

Thank you!

Gratitude

I have so much gratitude for the very special people
and businesses behind Nourish in 5, the book of my absolute
dreams that would not have been possible without them:

Ash, this book would not exist without you.

Ann from Organic Road, Natural Road and Go Vita Australia,
I'll forever be grateful for your support, love, nurturing and
all the countless opportunities you've given me.

13 Seeds, Cobram Estate, Well Naturally, Corn Thins,
& ENJO, for supporting my passions and this book.

Dale, Frank & Jenny from DaHa Project, for supporting
the book launch so so kindly and generously.

Weilynn, for your photography, patience and constant love +
encouragement. Marcus for his photography contribution also.

Meyland Media for his incredible recipe videography.

Shelby Koelewyn Design for the stunning graphic design
of this book, putting up with me and managing to do so
in a ridiculously short time frame that was given to us.

Lisa from OzHarvest, for being such a pleasure to work with.

Villa Rao Sassafras, for their wonderful hospitality and providing
the most aesthetic photography and videography backdrop.

Little Label Co, for transforming and organising my
pantry with your beautiful glass jars and vinyl labels.

You, the reader, whether you've been following the blog for a while
or you've recently discovered this book, words can't express how
incredibly grateful I am for your support of myself and OzHarvest
charity. I truly hope you enjoy and feel inspired by these pages
to nourish yourselves. Please do share any creations with me,
nothing makes me happier than sharing the love. :)

@AMYLEEACTIVE @NOURISH.in.5 on all Social Media platforms
Email hello@amyleeactive.com

CPSIA information can be obtained
at www.ICGtesting.com
Printed in the USA
LVHW070835111219
639879LV00013BA/107/P